LS-
GER
S|S|.

THE GLOBAL MANUFACTURING VANGUARD

THE GLOBAL MANUFACTURING VANGUARD

New Rules from the Industry Elite

MICHELINE MAYNARD

John Wiley & Sons, Inc.
New York • Chichester • Weinheim
Brisbane • Singapore • Toronto

Copyright © 1998 by Micheline Maynard. All rights reserved
Published by John Wiley & Sons, Inc.

Published simultaneously in Canada.

Library of Congress Cataloging-in-Publication Data:

Maynard, Micheline
    The global manufacturing vanguard : new rules from the industry
elite / Micheline Maynard.
        p.   cm.
    Includes bibliographical references and index.
    ISBN 0-471-18023-8 (alk. paper)
    1. Manufacturing industries.   2. Automobile industry and trade.
3. Industrial management.   4. International trade.   I. Title.
    HD9720.5.M39   1998
    658—dc21   97-49414
                                                                    CIP

Printed in the United States of America

10   9   8   7   6   5   4   3   2   1

To Frank and Lisa
and Maxine
with much love

Contents

Acknowledgments

Manufacturing plants have held a fascination for me since the first time I set foot in a factory. I was about seven years old, and my father thought it would be a fun summer excursion to visit Ford's massive Rouge complex in Dearborn, Michigan. Ford no longer gives these tours, and no wonder: The federal Occupational Safety and Health Administration would have a fit. Clinging to my father's hand, I walked along catwalks high above noisy, clattering machinery, the legs of my sunsuit billowing in the air current. A grime-covered man in hard hat and coveralls let me peer into a blast furnace deep in Ford's steel mill. I remember recoiling from the flames and heat, afraid I might be swallowed up by the molten metal, only to hear him laugh. "We lose a few (tourists) every year," he told my dad, who was trying to hide a smile.

What interested me most on that memorable afternoon was watching workers guide pieces of metal from overhead conveyer belts to the car bodies gliding by on the assembly line in front of them. One car was completed every 60 seconds, we were told, as we gazed on in awe. I couldn't grasp how a team of workers could put a Mustang together that fast until years later, when I realized that the measurement reflected only the end of final assembly.

As I began covering the auto industry as a reporter for United Press International, *U.S. News and World Report*, and Reuters, my interest in manufacturing grew. It wasn't until I joined *USA Today* in 1990, however, that I was able to fully indulge my fascination, thanks to the people I met at automotive, components, and other manufacturing companies who were eager to teach me about a specialty that had long lacked respect. In my years at *USA Today* I've been able to visit several dozen plants in all parts of the world and have learned something new at each one. For this book alone, I have conducted hundreds of hours of interviews, traveling from Europe to Latin America, and I've only begun scratching the surface of all there is to know about manufacturing.

In writing this book, one person stands out as having been my manufacturing godfather: Dennis Pawley, executive vice president at Chrysler Corporation. Over the past few years, Denny has spent hours with me, explaining his philosophy of manufacturing and the concepts of the Chrysler Operating System and suggesting plants for me to visit. He has been my bridge from the old "beat 'em, heat 'em, and ship 'em" days to the world of modern global manufacturing. My thanks also go to members of his staff, including Sham Rush-win, Frank Ewasyshyn, Jamie Bonini, and Don Manvel, and Chrysler's executive team, including Robert Eaton, Robert Lutz, Tom Gale, and François Castaing. I've also appreciated the help of Chrysler's public relations staff, including Arthur Liebler, Steve Harris, Tony Cervone, David Barnes, and Nicole Solomon.

I'm grateful to Toyota for its long history of assistance in my writing endeavors. Thanks go first to Mike DaPrile, vice president of manufacturing at Toyota's Georgetown, Kentucky, complex, whose willingness to meet with me over the years has been invaluable. Other thanks to individuals at Toyota go to Mikio Kitano, Alex Warren, Cheryl Jones, Hiroshi Okuda, Seizo Okamoto, Andy Wantunabe, Hajime Ohbe, and Dennis Cuneo. On Toyota's public relations staff, my appreciation especially goes to Barbara McDaniel, who made it possible for me to take part in Toyota's assessment program. Also, thanks to Jim Olson and John McCandless.

This book gave me the opportunity to conduct extensive research at two companies that I have come to deeply respect. At Cummins Engine, I thank James Henderson for his cooperation in this project and for letting me spend hours with his talented staff. Thanks also to Tim Solso, Kirin Patel, and Joseph Loughrey, as well as Margot Green and Ann Smith. At Dana Corporation, my appreciation goes to Southwood "Woody" Morcott, Jack Simpson, Gus Franklin, Czedo Eterovic, and Michael Laisure, as well as to Gary Corrigan.

At General Motors, thanks go to Jack Smith, the architect of GM's global strategy, who has always been willing to answer my probing if sometimes invasive questions. My appreciation also goes to Louis Hughes, Dave Herman, Peter Hanenberger, Mark Hogan, Mike Nylin, Eric Stephens, and Tom LaSorda, as well as to

GM's European public relations staff, including Ken Levy, HansPeter Ryser, and Karl Mauer. Also, I'd like to thank John Mueller and Alcione Viana. Sadly, two people who helped me with this project died before my book was completed. My thoughts go to the families of Dan Sallee and Bob Boroff.

I'd like to also thank a collection of my advisors, academicians, analysts, and other company executives. They include Joseph Phillippi, Steve Girsky, Greg Kagay, David Cole, Bill Lovejoy, David Gregory, James Womack, Alan Hammersmith, Anand Sharma, Pat Lancaster, Herb Brown, and Chihiro Nakao. In the labor movement, thanks go to Conrad Dowling, Larry Neihart, Mike Bennett, Buzz Hargrove, and Jane Armstrong.

I'd like to thank my editors at *USA Today*, starting with David Mazzarella, John Hillkirk, Rodney Brooks, and Paul Wiseman, and my auto team colleagues Jim Healey and Earle Eldridge, for their support. I also want to thank Bruce Rosenstein in the *USA Today* library. Thanks go to my agent, Russell Galen, and my editor at John Wiley & Sons, Jeanne Glasser, whose enthusiasm for this project has been a source of great encouragement.

Thanks go to my friends, scattered in all corners of the globe, including Judith Burns, Karla Vallance, Keith Naughton, Katie Kerwin, David Sedgwick, Martha Kinney, Brian and Rene Akre, Ellen Neuborne, T. J. Snyder, Bill Koenig, Ben Klayman, and Kevin Lahart. To those who have asked not to be identified by name, you have my deepest affection and appreciation for your unwavering support.

Finally, I'd like to thank my ever-patient family, my mother Bernice Maynard, my godmother, Maxine Clapper, my brother, Frank, his wife, Lisa, and of course, my adorable nephews, Benjamin and Parker.

Introduction

My manufacturing epiphany came on a dark, dismal, March day in 1996, shortly after I drove across the border between Austria and Hungary, on my way to visit yet another factory. So much snow had fallen in a freak late winter storm that the Austrian A2 *autobahn* that runs between Vienna and Graz had narrowed to just one lane of traffic. Cars and trucks crawled at a fraction of the usual 130-kilometers-an-hour pace. Normally, I would have flown down the road far faster than that, even at the risk of an expensive ticket and stern lecture from the highway *politzei*. What I thought would be a scenic two-hour trip from the outskirts of Vienna turned into a nerve-fraying four-hour journey.

Accustomed to sailing through checkpoints elsewhere in Europe, I was startled to see navy-uniformed guards at the Hungarian border prompting drivers to get out of their vehicles, open their trunks, and follow the officials inside low-slung office buildings. A young male guard stared at my U.S. passport and then at me through my rolled-down window as I stumbled to explain the reason for my visit to Hungary in recently learned, fundamental German.

"Opel? Why you go to Opel?" he replied in English. "To visit the engine plant in Szent Gotthard. I am a journalist," I explained. Shaking his head, he nonetheless carefully stamped my passport and handed it back, pointing to the road ahead. "Opel is there," he said, pointing to a road leading off to the right.

And it was. On the side of a two-lane country byway I spotted the familiar black, yellow, and white Opel logo that welcomed visitors to the newest factory in General Motors' mushrooming manufacturing empire. I had asked to come here simply because of my longtime fascination with manufacturing. This plant was crucial to central Europe and to GM. It marked GM's most significant investment yet in a developing market, and it was symbolic of Hungary's fledgling democracy. I was eager to see what an Opel plant behind the former Iron Curtain looked like, and I was curious to find out whether its workers had the abilities to tackle demanding factory jobs.

By this point in my career as a business journalist, I'd toured more than three dozen automotive components and consumer goods plants, from remote corners of Japan to urban centers in the United States, the industrial regions of Europe to dusty towns in Latin America. Executives who weren't comfortable in manufacturing environments often asked me, "How can you tell any of them apart? Don't they all look alike inside to you?" Tempted to tell them they would know what to look for if they spent more time in their own factories, my standard response had always been, "You learn something new at every plant you visit."

But at the Opel plant in Szent Gotthard, I learned more than I could have imagined. I discovered the underpinnings of what I would come to call the Global Manufacturing Vanguard.

Inside the plant, the only indication that I was standing in Hungary came from signs hanging from the ceiling above, written in consonant-laden Magyar. Pushing through a pair of swinging doors, I had a sensation similar to the scene in *The Wizard of Oz* when Dorothy steps out of her black-and-white cottage and into a full-color frame. Quickly I saw that Szent Gotthard was a manufacturing milestone—not for its high technology, like robots and automation, but rather for the sum of its parts.

Floors were clean. Aisles were wide. Parts inventory was arranged beside work stations in a neat and efficient manner that seemed straight out of a materials management seminar. The engine assembly line was laid out in half-moon shaped cells, each the territory of one of the factory's work teams trained to spot errors and come up with quick solutions. Hourly workers wore blue coveralls, managers donned lab coats, giving the factory the air of a high-tech research lab. On one section of the assembly line, the plant's manager was helping train a work team in the latest efficiency idea developed during a lean manufacturing seminar. Members of the team, which, I later learned, boasted three Ph.Ds, listened intently. Then each one gave the new process a try.

Deep inside the plant lay its nucleus: the computer

center. It was linked via Electronic Data Systems software to Opel's offices outside Frankfurt and to GM's offices in Warren, Michigan. With a keystroke, a manager could send e-mail requesting an update on the new layout GM was preparing for a still-empty portion of the plant, or provide up-to-the-minute sales figures on the cars that were being built from kits shipped to Szent Gotthard from elsewhere in the GM system.

Days before, I had visited GM's Aspern engine plant in Vienna, where its proud manager showed me the monumental improvements in quality that were coming from the factory's embrace of lean manufacturing. That plant had been built in 1964; it sprawled for acres, requiring a golf-cart guided tour. The Szent Gotthard plant, opened just two years before my visit, was compact, easy to walk in a single morning. Yet production at the two plants was almost identical, about 500,000 engines a year.

Exhilaration swept through me as I drove away from the Hungarian factory. That plant could have been built anywhere, I thought—in the United States, in Germany, in Japan, or in Brazil. The equipment was as modern and the layout as efficient as anything in any engine plant I'd ever seen. Those managers could walk into any factory at any company in the world and do their jobs. Those workers had more education and were even better trained than people on assembly lines in the United States. Hearing my reaction as we met in his office in Zurich, GM Europe manufacturing executive Mike Nylin smiled. "You're going to see a lot more Hungarys," he told me. He was right.

Over the next two years, as I conducted research for this book. I felt the same way in plants in Kaiserslauten, Germany; Hiroshima, Japan; Rosario, Argentina; Osasco, Brazil; Shelbyville, Kentucky; and Columbus, Indiana. My manufacturing godfathers told me that I had learned to look at factories with "lean eyes," recognizing efficient layouts at a glance. But I was seeing something more. I began to understand that plants like these, and the managers whose vision had created them, are emblematic of a handful of companies that are setting new and dynamic standards for a global manufacturing environment that is exploding with competition.

1

The Global Manufacturing Vanguard

In the 1990s, "going global" has become a corporate mantra. CEOs like GM's Jack Smith end speeches by exhorting their corporate troops to "Think Global!" even when their employees are hundreds of miles from the nearest border. Every morning, broadcasters on CNBC, CNN, and the BBC punctuate their financial news reports with word of the latest mergers joining international players, joint ventures linking companies and governments, and developments in key world markets. Every afternoon, journalists at newspapers from the *Financial Times* to the *Wall Street Journal* are at work in Europe, the United States, and Asia, writing about moves affecting each and every continent.

To be sure, companies have been going global for

centuries. The economies of China, England, and Holland long depended on trade in markets as far-flung as the United States, Africa, and Indonesia. Yet, as late as the mid-1980s, most of the world's companies stubbornly clung to the idea that dominance in their home markets was their primary mission. They battled to keep exports from eating into their market share. The United States and European countries banded together to limit Japanese auto sales, never reckoning that companies like Toyota, Nissan, and Honda would get around quotas by building plants in their backyards.

The confluence of two events awakened the business world to the opportunities that global markets offered. One was the fall of the Berlin Wall in 1989. The boisterous students who chipped down the graffiti-covered blocks of concrete separating East and West Germany did more than open up a border. They gave world relevance to countries long thought of as mere dots on a map dominated by the Soviet Union. In the same way, the tragic events at Beijing's Tiananmen Square, broadcast to millions of world viewers earlier that year, woke up people around the globe to the realization that China was not a one-dimensional nation of people who would blindly follow their leaders' directives. It opened business leaders' eyes to the reality that many Chinese people were willing to face choices, such as democracy over communism, and that they would use the modern weapons of technology, including television and fax machines, to make their voices heard. The episode also made Chinese leaders realize they no longer had the power to shut off their country from the western world, and that one of their own most valuable weapons, both politically and economically, would be to offer business opportunities to foreign investors.

Coming just months apart, the Berlin Wall's collapse

and the events in China were the triggers that set off a yet-unrelenting exploration by the world's major companies of potential new markets. Many executives agreed wholeheartedly with Louis Hughes, President of GM's International Operations, who urged his company to push forward with international investments in the early 1990s even in the wake of near-bankruptcy at home. "There is only a short window of opportunity to do this," Hughes declares. They, like GM, set off like global prospectors, panning for golden opportunites.

The best of these adventuresome companies make up what I call the Global Manufacturing Vanguard, a collection of perhaps no more than a dozen firms from around the world that are dictating the future of manufacturing. Merriam Webster's Collegiate Dictionary, Tenth Edition, defines the word *vanguard* as "the forefront of an action or movement." It is the single best term to describe these companies, who are setting a pace for others to attempt to match.

While other companies are still grappling with downsizing at home as they try to expand overseas, firms like Toyota, Cummins Engine Company, General Electric, Chrysler, Dana, and other members of the Vanguard have become multinational, with a management that is multicultural. For them, home markets have become, primarily, a place to put a headquarters. These organizations may select one language in which to communicate, but the concepts, phrases, and guiding principles they use can be understood by employees in all parts of their operations.

Although Vanguard CEOs might occasionally step up to podiums to rant about unfair trading practices in a particular country such as Korea or India, the leaders of these companies know that such battles are no longer their overriding concern. The game is no longer the

United States versus Japan, Europe versus Asia, Brazil versus Argentina. Every part of the world offers opportunities, some of which are strategic, such as being first to invest when a country embraces democracy, as GM did by entering eastern Germany with its Eisenach plant. Some opportunities represent the potential for easy sales growth among newly prosperous consumers, such as Thailand before its recent economic problems, whereas others might be a mere public relations ploy today but a valuable foot in the door tomorrow.

Vanguard companies have banished the phrase "We can't do business there because. . . ." To the Vanguard, no market is too expensive, no consumer is undesireable, no trade barriers are too daunting, and no location is too remote. It is not because these companies are reckless. It is because a willingness to take calculated risks is a part of their corporate cultures. This might seem to describe companies known in business circles as "world class." Yet members of the Vanguard are beyond world class. They are combining outstanding manufacturing systems (that don't necessarily use the latest technology) with ultraclear values and the determination to be successful. These companies have dashed the notion that the future of manufacturing lies solely in space-age clean rooms, where silicon is etched in minute amounts onto circuit boards. While all have well-run factories, these are just the tip of an iceberg that extends deep into a sea of excellence. Says Southwood "Woody" Morcott, CEO of Toledo-based automotive components maker Dana Corporation, "I'm not sure we've ever endorsed the notion of global manufacturing. What we're looking for is global business and the manufacturing plan will follow. You want an organization that's globally focused and globally thinking."

Size is not a determining factor for Vanguard companies. For the most part, Vanguard members are not the largest companies in their industries, and neither are all of them financial powerhouses. Vanguard companies are as small as Cummins, with $5 billion a year in annual sales, and as large as Toyota, whose annual revenues are 20 times greater. Rather than succeeding solely through financial clout, Vanguard companies' commitment to global manufacturing is demonstrated by constancy and consistency in every process and every person in every part of the globe.

Who are these people behind the Vanguard companies? Some are corporate celebrities, such as GE Chief Executive Jack Welch, whose every visionary thought seems destined to be e-mailed across the corporate landscape within minutes of its utterance. Though Welch has actually been shifting GE's focus away from manufacturing for the past decade, he exemplifies the type of bold leadership that members of the Vanguard display. In Japan, Toyota CEO Hiroshi Okuda stands out as an unconventional executive who can cause a plant manager to snap into action with a single offhand comment. Percy Barnevik, head of Sweden's Investor ABB, is a European manufacturing figure whose personal clout and quotability far outweigh his engineering company's reach.

Some others are best known in their own manufacturing arenas, such as Dana's Morcott, a courtly yet steely-eyed executive famous for correcting visitors who refer to Dana as a North American company, or Chrysler Executive Vice President Dennis Pawley, who sought advice from Toyota to fix the flaws in his company's plants. Just as vital are the insiders who are heroes only in their own home towns, such as Larry Neihart, former president of the Dieselworkers Union, whose willingness to break with tradition led to an unprecedented 11-year contract that gave Cummins the labor peace it needed at home to pursue a global quest, or Cheryl Jones, the former Kroger grocery store manager now entrusted with a key piece of Toyota's North American manufacturing empire.

All of these people have learned what it is like to compete in a highly charged environment that second-rate companies still have trouble recognizing, let alone embracing. Singly and collectively, from corporate suite to factory floor, they have come to the realization that manufacturing is of paramount importance in the chain of events that leads from idea to customer. Says Peter Hanenberger, who directs GM's international technical development, "Our philosophy is clear. Without manufacturing, nothing is possible. If you want to be a successful company, you must be a manufacturing company, not only a design and engineering company."

Adds Cummins Engine CEO James Henderson, "[Cummins management] is responsible not only for the character and honesty of the business, but the people end of the business. There is a built-in understanding that if we are all together, we can accomplish much more than if we are not." In this realization, Cummins's executives and union leaders have the support of company employees and union members, who know the price that international competition can exact.

Vanguard companies are populated with experienced global veterans and up-and-coming managers being trained to lead in a global atmosphere. Free from the traditions that funneled all decisions to the top, they are trusting their employees and factory workers with responsibilities that once fell only to those in management jobs. They are setting down extraordinary requirements, such as Dana's dictate that senior managers hold at least five different types of jobs, including an international post, during their careers, and Toyota's difficult assessment process for prospective hourly workers, which requires them to spend four excruciating hours on a mock assembly line and participate in team-building exercises that have brought some applicants to blows in the classroom.

Joining the Vanguard is not the result of a decision made quickly with the expectation of instant results. Going global, to these companies, is not a flavor of the month. In mid-1997, GM faced a near-revolution by its European engineers, who were cracking from the strain of developing cars for Europe, helping design next-generation vehicles for the United States, and shouldering responsibility for the vehicles GM was selling in all its developing markets. The resulting uproar made international headlines for months, forcing GM to defend its global strategy and to admit it had not communicated its ideas clearly to its employees and to the public.

Says GM CEO Jack Smith, "As we go global—and we are committed to running global—change is involved. Change is difficult for any organization when something new occurs. It's going to create some tension. It's hard to accept why that change has taken place. People are comfortable with the way that things exist. But change is inevitable. And when we do it right, I think people are going to understand why." Asked if GM would abandon its globalization drive in face of the complaints, Smith says simply, "We can't."

Smith's determination exemplifies the focus that Vanguard companies must demonstrate. Even GM, for all its financial clout and global reach, has not yet joined the top ranks of global competitors owing to continued problems in the U.S. and Europe that have not yet been fully addressed. Smith would be the first to agree, however, that the quest is not a 100-yard dash but an unending marathon. Relaxing at this stage of the race means being trampled by the runners coming up from behind.

It's hard to tell who fired the starting pistol on this global race, because companies have been expanding beyond their home markets literally for centuries. Philip Morris actually started as a cigarette shop in London in 1847 and began producing cigarettes in the United States around 1910. Mercedes Benz's plant in Vance, Alabama, which opened in the summer of 1997, is actually the company's second attempt at building cars in the United States: Piano maker Steinway assembled the first Mercedes made outside of Germany in New York in the early 1900s. Many of the biggest names in U.S. manufacturing, such as General Motors, General Electric, Procter & Gamble, and Ford, were launching global ventures in the 1920s, thanks to the nation's economic prosperity at that time. Even so, these international operations almost always took a backseat to the companies' emphasis on their home markets.

When companies hit financial potholes, their foreign operations still are often the first to be jettisoned. Congress ordered Chrysler to dump its investments in Latin America and Europe in 1980 as a condition for $5 billion in federal loan guarantees; Brazil and Argentina abound with companies now reentering their markets after the dismal economic days of the 1980s and early 1990s, when inflation averaged 2,000 percent a month. Roger Smith, GM's CEO in the 1980s, was distinctly North American-focused, despite his ground-breaking joint ventures with Japanese companies like Toyota and Isuzu. In 1986, he sent Jack Smith to Europe to find a buyer for GM's money-losing operations there.

Instead of arranging a sale, Jack Smith convinced his boss it might be a wise idea to remain in the world's second-largest car market. He then plunged into an overhaul plan. If he had not, GM would now lack the technological base from which it is launching its own global drive into markets such as China, Thailand, and Poland.

Companies whose international operations were begun after World War II have often taken a different approach. Japanese companies are much more likely than their U.S. and European counterparts to have a targeted global expansion strategy. Sony was among the first companies whose name became synonymous with global strength, and for good reason. Akio Morita deliberately changed the company's name in the late 1950s from Tokyo Tsushin Kogyo to Sony because he wanted a name that would be easy to remember and easy to pronounce around the world. Sony's bankers had opposed the name change, saying the company had spent 10 years developing its original brand name.

But Morita says, "Although our company was small and we saw Japan as quite a large and potentially active market, it became obvious to me that if we did not set our sights on marketing abroad, we could not grow into the kind of company [we] had envisioned." Sony's goal was to change the image of Japanese products from cheap and flimsy to innovative and desirable. To do so, Sony was on the leading edge of Japanese manufacturers who set up factories in the United States in order to be closer to their customers. It opened its first electronics factory in San Diego in 1969, hiring U.S. managers to run the facility. Other Japanese electronics companies followed suit. "It was a pretty typical plant. They were just leveraging their brand name and their product technology," says James Womack, coauthor of

The Machine That Changed the World, a groundbreaking book that illuminated Japanese companies' seemingly inscrutable manufacturing techniques. "The next step was to bring a manufacturing process plus product technology," he says.

That came through automakers, whom Womack considers to be particularly important players in any country's drive to attract foreign companies because of the capital they invest, the engineering and design resources they use, and the attention their products attract. Japan's influx was led by Honda, which gambled that U.S. customers would be willing to buy cars from a company that was best known for making motor scooters and lawn mowers. At home, investors and consumers were hooting at Honda's audacity in challenging more established players like Toyota and Nissan. In Japan, Honda is still only the fourth-largest automaker, in part because it would not spend the money to develop the extensive dealership networks that its biggest competitors have.

Honda's decision to open a car plant in Marysville, Ohio, in 1982 kicked off a new chapter in global manufacturing. It was not the first such "transplant" factory by a foreign auto company in the United States. Germany's Volkswagen, which has always been an aggressive player on the global scene, preceded Honda by four years with a factory in Westmoreland, Pennsylvania, in 1978. Volkswagen's U.S. plant actually came after its first factory in China, and well after its Beetle had become the best-selling foreign car in the United States. Both Honda and VW were taking advantage of two energy shortages that had sent U.S. consumers scrambling for high-quality, fuel-efficient cars, which Detroit had failed to produce. By the time VW opened Westmoreland, consumers were standing 10 deep in showrooms vying for its Rabbits, later replaced by Golfs. No one forced VW to open a factory in the United States; in fact, Detroit automakers feared VW's invasion because it would potentially increase the company's capacity to produce cars that Detroit could not provide.

But when Honda opened Marysville—brought to Ohio by then Governor John Rhodes for a mere $5 million in incentives—Japanese carmakers held nearly 35 percent of the U.S. car market, all of it in exports. Officials in Detroit and Washington told the Japanese to build factories in the United States or else face strict import restrictions. The United States and Japan, in fact, had agreed to so-called voluntary import restraints that limited the number of cars Japan could bring into the United States to 2 million vehicles a year. In retrospect, the calls for Japanese production in the United States may have done more damage to U.S. automakers than the proponents ever anticipated. Since Honda's arrival, Japanese automakers have invested $14 billion in U.S. factories, far more than Big Three auto executives ever dreamed they would spend outside their home market. Nearly 70 percent of the 3.4 million vehicles sold in the United States each year by Japanese companies are built in the United States

Quickly Honda was followed by a pair of U.S.–Japanese joint ventures between General Motors and Toyota and between Chrysler and Mitsubishi. Nissan opened a plant in Smyrna, Tennessee, and Subaru and Isuzu joined forces in West Lafayette, Indiana. Eventually, Toyota also built a plant on its own, buying 10,000 acres of horse pasture in Georgetown, Kentucky, outside Lexington to create what would become one of the world's most admired manufacturing complexes. In 1997, more than 5,000 executives, consultants, researchers, journalists, and academics traveled to Toy-

ota's Georgetown plant to study Toyota's transformation from the most Japanese of automakers to the most
global of companies. At Georgetown, more than 7,500
nonunion workers turn out Toyota Camry and Avalon
sedans and Sienna minivans, using the same Toyota
Production System processes the company uses in
Japan and elsewhere in the world.

These workers earn wages comparable to their counterparts in Detroit auto plants, about $18 an hour, yet
they have few job classifications, participate in making
their tasks more efficient, and have the ability to stop
the assembly line when they see problems. Seeing Toyota's success, Mercedes decided to try the same approach in Alabama, now the only production site in the
world for its super-popular M-class sport utility. Combined, non-U.S. companies now employ 50,000 workers at their U.S. auto factories, which are among the
world's leading examples of manufacturing expertise.

The other end of the manufacturing continuum lies
several thousand miles away, just over the U.S.-Mexico
border, in Tijuana, Mexico. Here, 5,000 Mexicans earning about $1.20 a day assemble large-screen color TVs
and computer monitors from U.S.-made components,
shipped duty-free from the United States Sony's plant
is among 2,000 such *maquiladora* factories, which produce everything from Volkswagen's new Beetle to
clothing, furniture, and electronic goods. More than
600,000 Mexican workers have jobs in plants owned by
foreign companies drawn to Mexico for its cheap labor
rates and ready supply of workers. In a country with
about 30 percent unemployment, the *maquiladoras* have
provided millions of dollars in tax revenues to the Mexican government, which made production in Mexico a
prerequisite for any company wanting to sell its products there.

On the surface, it seems an easy trade-off: cheap labor for a company's products in return for market access. Yet the *maquiladoras* also exemplify the problems that global manufacturers have encountered in developing markets elsewhere in the world. Turnover is constant because employees often prefer to risk crossing into the United States in search of higher wages. Human rights groups in manufacturers' home countries denounce the plants' long working hours. Unions such as the United Auto Workers are trying to organize the workers, and some plants have been hit by strikes. These factors are prompting some manufacturers to consider sites deeper into Mexico's interior, which is not so industrialized. There, too, manufacturers face a paradox: The cheap labor that has drawn them to invest in Mexico may not have the education necessary to understand a manufacturing process or to handle sensitive components. And it might not be easy to find a manager in the United State, Europe, or Japan who wants to move his or her family to Mexico's interior to run the plant.

As U.S. manufacturers have learned just by crossing their own border, the pitfalls of global manufacturing are numerous. Yet companies are pressing into new markets, from Brazil and Argentina to Thailand, India, China, and Africa, joined in this great global rush by competitors from all corners of the world. The best of these companies, members of the Global Manufacturing Vanguard, are well prepared for the journey because they see it as one that is making their companies stronger. They know that globalization demands new ways of thinking that require them to be less rigid, less focused on the home market, and more open to new cultures and new concepts.

Says University of Michigan professor William Lovejoy, "For the first 100 years after the Industrial Revolution, firms organized as a hierarchical bureaucracy, patterned after the military. Once you bureaucratize, you can achieve the task at hand, but it doesn't make you very good at flexibility or growth. Now, we're looking for a new dominant organization. Everyone is experimenting." And members of the Global Manufacturing Vanguard are charting the course.

2

The Building Blocks

Throughout the 1990s, countless hours and millions of dollars in consulting fees have been spent trying to answer a very simple question: How can a company turn a collection of manufacturing plants around the world into a seamless global operation?

The answer indicates the subtle yet tangible difference between the ranks of superregional players and members of the Global Manufacturing Vanguard. When other companies were just beginning to realize the need to go global, Vanguard members were already well along on implementing a strategy to put them in the front of the pack. When other companies were puzzling over ways to shake up their internally competitive culture, Vanguard members had already begun blending the best aspects of other cultures into their own corporate fabric. When other companies were trying to figure out how to convince wary managers to take overseas assignments, Vanguard members had already made international experience a prerequisite to executive success.

No matter their size or the location of their home base, Vanguard companies share a set of fundamental building blocks that form the foundation for their success. All of these building blocks are critical. All must be present before a company can hope to enter the fast lane of global competition.

These fundamental building blocks are

- Executive vision and demonstrated success in executing that vision
- Financial strength, including a disciplined balance sheet, market success at home and overseas, and clearly defined measurements for global ventures
- Resources, from people to technology

Says General Electric CEO Jack Welch: "We have every intention of outperforming the global business environment. We have the businesses and the people and the capital resources to do that. Shame on us if we don't."[1]

EXECUTIVE VISION

Vanguard members agree: a global strategy must start at the top. It is the responsibility of top management to articulate a global plan and make sure that it is understood and implemented throughout the company, from top managers to hourly workers. "Have a reason and then do it right. Create an atmosphere and lay down the rules of management behavior. That is the best you can do,"[2] says Percy Barnevik, former chief executive of Swiss engineering firm ABB Asea Brown Bovera, who became CEO of Sweden's Investor conglomerate in mid-1997.

"The first key is to have a clear vision of what your company means by *global*," says Eric Stephens, executive director of lean manufacturing implementation at General Motors' International Operations. "Certainly, there may be discussion on the 'how' but not a lot of debate on what we mean." Consistent direction and reinforcement from the top is crucial to an organization's embracing a global mission. The 1990s saw the emergence of the first generation of global CEOs who had spent time outside their companies' home markets. As the twenty-first century begins, these internationally trained leaders are likely to become the norm, not the exception. Their global experience has taught them to react quickly to problems, which are considered to be opportunities, and to push their organizations to think the same way. As author James Womack puts it, "Imagine you're in a jumbo jet that's a thousand seats abreast and a thousand seats deep. The guys sitting at the two window seats might say, 'Hey we're about to collide with Mount Everest!' But in the middle [of the plane passengers are] saying, 'Hey, we're doing fine, when are they going to serve dinner?' "

Added the late Cuban-born Coca-Cola Chief Executive Roberto Goizueta, "You find a lot of companies that say, 'Our business is global,' but then in their lexicon, they talk about 'international sales.' A U.S. [multinational company] tends to view the U.S. as its base and to export from there. A global company produces locally and markets locally around the world."[3] Coca-

Cola is a case in point: Seventy percent of its sales come from outside the United States. Its soft drinks are bottled in such far-flung corners as Venezuela, Russia, and Italy and are sold virtually everywhere—even, despite a 35-year U.S. embargo, in Cuban grocery stores.

Every Vanguard company's worldwide manufacturing push has been clearly defined and explained and repeatedly articulated by senior management. Like Coca-Cola, most Vanguard companies began implementing global operations long before the competition caught on to the opportunity the global marketplace represents. Dana Chief Executive Southwood "Woody" Morcott, whose company now has plants in 30 countries, with 48,000 employees, first defined his company's globalization thrust in 1990. He created a 10-year plan and gave it the label Dana 2000. Now, says Morcott, "2000"-named plans are clichés. But at the time, "we were the very first company where I saw the term '2000' used. It was a focal point that people could relate to. It looked like *Star Wars*," Morcott says.

Morcott already had his own set of building blocks to work from in the company's operating philosophy, which is called the Dana Style. Easily condensed into a one-page brochure, the Dana Style is a set of nine clearly defined company goals, including earnings, growth, people, planning, organization, quality, customers, communication, and citizenship. At another company, the brochure might be tucked into a drawer and forgotten. Not at Dana. Anyone who spends any time talking with Morcott or his executives and managers around the world hears the Dana Style reflected in every aspect of the business. Traits for which Dana has become known, such as requiring two ideas per month from every employee, are part of the Dana Style. So is the company's organizational structure, which limits levels of management to just five, from factory floor to regional president. Likewise, Dana's declaration that its workers are experts within their 25-square-feet of work space is part of the philosophy as well. With the guiding principles of the Dana Style in hand, Morcott built the framework for his global drive.

His primary target was to double Dana's $5 billion in annual revenue to $10 billion by the year 2000. To reach that goal, Morcott wanted Dana's non-U.S. revenue to climb from 26 percent to 50 percent of the company's overall sales. At the time, Dana was already the largest independent automotive and industrial components maker in the United States, outdistanced only by parts subsidiaries at General Motors and Ford. But overseas, Dana was being challenged at every turn by aggressive German and Japanese companies such as GKN, Bosch, and Denso, who vied with Dana for business in various parts of the world. Without a global focus, Morcott knew Dana would forever be pigeonholed as an "American" parts supplier. That label would create problems for Dana in trying to convince its customers that it could handle their business in international markets.

Says Georgia-born Morcott, "You have to decide, when do you start using the term 'global' and when do you stop defining it as an American company with international operations?" Dana's Chief Financial Officer, Jack Simpson, adds that the embrace of the word *global* was meant as a clear signal to employees that Dana was serious about attempting a broader push. "Dana's not a faddish company. We don't jump on the bandwagon, starry-eyed, willy-nilly, just because it's the in thing," Simpson says.

Dana shifted focus well ahead of the major U.S. automakers, General Motors, Ford, and Chrysler, to which it supplies parts, and with which it competes for some parts business. None of those companies began seriously implementing their own global plans until the mid-1990s.

But Morcott points out that Dana serves not only the Big Three U.S. companies but 28 of the world's 30 major auto companies, from Toyota to Mercedes, Kia to Chrysler. "If a vehicle is being manufactured anywhere in the world, we want to be there to supply it. Large suppliers like ourselves are often more global than the manufacturers. [The manufacturers] look at a market first as a place to supply vehicles. Then they have to look at the competitive conditions, the size of the market, whether or not to make a major investment. We look at the total market." In doing so, Dana is able to gauge market potential around the world. Says Dana President Joseph Magliochetti, "All of our customers are talking about growing globally. We have got to think out ahead of them."

One example of Dana's success is its operation in Brazil. In 1996 and 1997, the world's major automakers announced investments in Brazil worth nearly $20 billion collectively. By the mid-1990s, Dana already had 21 plants in Brazil, plus 4 in nearby Argentina, and 18 more scattered across Latin America. Dana's 1996 Latin American sales were $600 million, and Morcott thinks they could hit $1.5 billion by the year 2000, despite economic troubles that struck Brazil in late 1997.

Simply staking out a claim for 50 percent non-U.S. business was one thing; getting there required focus. Under Dana 2000, the company decided to define its core businesses and realign its operations worldwide to reflect those priorities. It settled on eight core operations: axles, driveshafts, structural components such as vehicle frames, sealing products, filters, engine components, industrial products, and leasing services. It also designated four world regions—Europe, North America, Latin America, and Asia—where it would focus on producing those products. The businesses and regions are aligned in a two-dimensional matrix: Each core business has a "product parent" or senior executive who is responsible for overseeing design, development, and production. Each region has its own president charged with dealing with customers, finding new markets, and defining strategic opportunities. Every product parent and every regional president frequently confer via meetings, video conferences, and e-mail, sharing information and getting advice. Morcott is out there, too, hammering home Dana's priorities in frequent visits to the company's far-flung plants. A three-week trip in early 1997 took him to 17 plants in the United States, Brazil, and Europe.

The two-dimensional setup immediately clarified Dana's strengths and weaknesses. In 1990, only half of its businesses were manufacturing those core products. By 1997, that number had risen to more than 75 percent. By the year 2000, says company president Magliochetti, "we'd like for 90 percent of our business to be in our core products, embodied by our core values, managed regionally as well as globally." The remaining 10 percent is designated for emerging businesses that offer opportunities for future growth.

Morcott often cites one example of how the twin focus has enhanced Dana's global approach. Although the company had settled on axles as one of its core businesses, it did not have a single European axle plant in 1990. Seven years later, it has 11 axle plants there, thanks to acquisitions, joint ventures, and expansions. Says Magliochetti: "Our aim is to become a global company that is responsive to regional needs."

Morcott says the two-dimensional setup "is working marvelously well. That's why we've had this spurt of growth." Magliochetti notes that one byproduct has been speed. "We've learned enough so that 15 people in a room can decide what needs to be done, and it's done," Magliochetti says. Even if that room is in Dana's colonial-looking Toledo, Ohio, headquarters, executives sitting at the conference table have no doubt where Dana's direction lies. Says Modular Systems Vice President Michael Laisure, "The world's our market." By focusing on core products and key markets, Dana has cut its corporate staff in Toledo from 400 people to 84. Such slim ranks might seen anorexic at a less-focused company. But all those Dana staffers have spent years working together, linked by Dana's emphatic promote-from-within policy that rewards performance and loyalty with advancement.

Toyota CEO Hiroshi Okuda is pushing his company to pick up its pace as well—even though competitors around the world are often left breathless trying to keep up with the Japanese auto giant. Okuda readily acknowledges that the manufacturing world universally holds up Toyota as the premier example of a global organization. "I would have to agree that we are the best," he says in his usual blunt fashion. But that isn't good enough for Toyota's tradition-smashing president, who has repeatedly voiced his desire to make the auto giant a leaner, faster-moving player.

Weeks after he was named Toyota president in 1995, Okuda embarked on a $13.5 billion globalization drive unrivaled in world business. "In all sorts of areas, a big change is going on sharply and quickly," Okuda declared in his plan, called the "Great Leap Forward." When Okuda's plan has been fully implemented, Toyota will have firmly planted roots in a range of global markets. From North America to Europe and from Latin America to Asia, six new factories are planned or are in the process of being built, all of them devised according to the Toyota Production System, a set of values and processes virtually identical in all its global plants. In 1998 alone, Toyota plans to open new plants in Indiana, West Virginia, and Brazil.

The products those plants will be producing represent a departure from Toyota's previous pattern. While other companies are still trying to pick out the countries around the globe where they want to operate, Okuda is focusing on the products he will build in this vast global empire. Since the end of World War II, Toyota has made its name on high-quality but largely anonymous looking cars, designed in Japan for Japanese consumers and subsequently exported to other markets. Even when Toyota began building cars in places like California and England, the vehicles it produced overseas were generally carbon copies of those it built at home. The word "innovation" was rarely heard. Not anymore.

Today, leading-edge vehicles are joining Toyota's lineup, such as the Sienna minivan in North America and the budget-priced Solona sedan in Asia. In addition, Toyota is taking a new turn with its old standby, the Corolla compact, sold in all of its major world markets. Toyota wants Corolla to be seen not as a Japanese compact but as a car that reflects buyers' tastes in world markets. Corollas for Japan, the United States, and Europe all share similar underpinnings but have different exterior sheet metal and interior features, depending on what buyers want. General Motors is hoping to implement a similar strategy with its small cars in the United States and Europe. But the first of GM's cars won't be ready until 2002. By then, Toyota will already be putting the finishing touches on its second generation of global cars designed to meet local buyers' needs. Says Toyota division General Manager J. Davis Illingworth, "The target just moved."

One of Okuda's goals for these cars is to speed up their development time, clocked from the point when Toyota's board funds the project to the time the vehicle hits showrooms. Toyota is already the auto industry's world leader in product development time, needing only 24 months to complete a car project. That is nearly eight months faster than U.S. leader Chrysler and 22 months faster than GM's average. Yet Okuda, relaxing in an armchair during a 1997 interview at Toyota's newly expanded Cambridge, Ontario, factory, shakes his head.

"That isn't fast enough," he declares. His worldwide goal: 18 months. And that's only for Toyota's most important volume sellers, such as the Camry sedan and the 4Runner sport utility. Okuda thinks limited-edition vehicles, like sports cars and luxury coupes, ought to hit the streets months faster. One way he expects to meet this goal is by a determined focus on cost-cutting. Toyota was already known for the efficiency of its factories when Okuda took charge, but in his years as president, it has found ways to slice $2.5 billion in spending. Okuda is pushing managers to come up with $800 million in cuts every year for the foreseeable future. One such program looks at the underbody of a car and how Toyota can eliminate the steps required to produce it. Okuda sees such leanness as the basis for the "Great Leap Forward" he wants to take into the global manufacturing arena, propelling Toyota even further ahead of its rivals.

Nearly all of Toyota's expansion has taken place under its own steam. As one of the world's richest companies, with a $20 billion cash cushion, it can easily afford to fund its own expansion. Not so for Indiana's Cummins Engine Company, a maker of engines and industrial power equipment, which encountered severe financial turbulence a decade ago before it hit on a global approach as its key to survival. Hammered by competition from Japanese engine makers and a resurgent Detroit Diesel, Cummins was in bad shape when the 1990s began. It had lost money every year from 1987 through 1991, forcing it to slash its dividend and let thousands of workers go as it struggled to stay competitive in its main arena, diesel engines for heavy duty trucks. Cummins's weakness made it a perpetual takeover target, causing numerous sleepless nights among employees and managers in its picturesque headquarters town of Columbus, Indiana.

But Cummins fought back by overhauling itself and by joining forces with some of its toughest rivals. Today, the $5.5 billion company has 40 plants stretching from England to India and from Brazil to Japan, many of them joint ventures. It has become the leading example of how a relatively small company can prosper in a global setting by carefully selecting its partners and focusing clearly on what it wants to achieve.

"There is great value in partnering with a respected organization," says Cummins CEO James Henderson, whose direct gaze and uncomplicated manner bring to mind a middle-aged Jimmy Stewart. "One, it can help defray cost. Two, it can be good technically." In 1993, this philosophy bore significant fruit. In October of that year, then-Cummins President Henderson traveled to Hawaii, where he and Tetsuya Katada, president of Japanese engine manufacturer Komatsu, agreed to a joint venture linking their operations in North America and Japan.

The deal reflected a sharp contrast to Cummins's

anger in the 1980s at Komatsu's attempts to steal its customers by slashing prices up to 30 percent. Struggling Cummins had been forced to match the price cuts. To raise $250 million in badly needed cash, it had to sell a one-third stake of the company to three manufacturers—Ford Motor Company, Tenneco, Inc., and Kubota Corporation of Japan. Cummins officials were unnerved by Komatsu's barely concealed strategy to drive earth-moving equipment maker Caterpillar into the ground, with a "Circle Cat" strategy aimed at every market where Caterpillar did business. Some executives wondered if Komatsu might ultimately be planning the same type of subterfuge with Cummins.

Yet communications remained open between Cummins and Komatsu. The two companies had first talked in the 1960s about sharing licensing rights on various products. In 1996, three years after joint venture talks began, Komatsu agreed to build Cummins's B-series engine, used on pickup trucks and boats, at its joint venture plant, now called Komatsu Cummins, in Oyama, Japan. Meanwhile, Cummins said it would produce Komatsu's 30-liter engine at the Cummins Komatsu venture in Seymour, Indiana. Work began at both plants that same year.

In addition to resolving their animosity, each side felt it had won something from the venture: Komatsu got technical help from Cummins in meeting increasingly strict diesel engine emissions standards that have been adopted in various world markets. Cummins's expertise meant Komatsu did not have to do its own engineering. Meanwhile, Cummins got a foot in the door in Japan with engines that it also sells in other Asian countries. The deal came just a few months after Cummins made arrangements with India's Tata Engineering and Locomotive Company (TELCO) to build a jointly owned plant in Jamshadpur, about 150 miles west of Calcutta. The $90 million deal put Cummins years ahead of its competition in a market now seen as one of the world's most promising.

Says Henderson, "If you look at market expansion joint ventures, you can go about it in two ways. In places like China and India, you can go it alone and fight it out. Or you can choose a partner who already has a manufacturing base to whom you can offer technology. If we can ally, we can end up with strong local market knowledge and a base of operations. We have been both fortunate and given a lot of thought to how you do business internationally."

Cummins's global push is far from over, says Henderson. "We say we're global, but certainly in many cases other companies are stronger than we are. I'm impressed with where we are but we still have (work) in front of us. It's one thing to get a beach head but it's another to establish strong organizations. I like to think our job is just starting."

FINANCIAL STRENGTH

It is human nature to try to "get it right the next time." And that is the excuse that many manufacturers are using to justify their global expansion drives. In their home markets, they claim, their competitiveness is hampered by any combination of factors, such as market saturation, uncooperative unions, high transportation costs, government red tape, and narrow profit margins. But elsewhere, the sun is shining. For minimal investments, companies promise their new international ventures will bring double-digit returns, due to cheaper labor, government incentives, and markets

filled with consumers who've never before been offered such sophisticated goods. There is evidence to
back up these perceptions: Over the past 10 years,
North American industrial markets have seen an overall growth rate of 6.5 percent, while Europe has grown
at about 10 percent a year, Latin America at about 14
percent a year, and Asia at 18 percent a year.

Yet the arguments make author James Womack sigh
in frustration. "Why don't we think about taking out
waste, rather than building something in the jungle?"
he asks.

Vanguard companies have already beaten him to
the punch. For them, financial strength is a prerequisite
to expanding globally. It is not financial strength expressed merely by size but by measurements across the
company. "Without the financial resources, it's difficult
to even ponder the notion of being a global company,"
says Dana Chief Financial Officer Jack Simpson.

"The core must be very, very healthy, with good
strong cash flows and good returns before you start to
deploy those resources, both human and capital, to
other areas of the world," Simpson adds.

How big is big enough to go global? To hear General
Motors (GM) Chief Financial Officer J. Michael Losh
tell it, companies smaller than the Fortune 15 don't
stand a chance. "You ask yourself, who's best positioned to become a global company? It's we, Ford and
Toyota," he told Wall Street analysts in early 1997. Even
if Losh was speaking only about the world's auto companies, let alone other manufacturers, his is far too narrow a view.

Cummins has joined the Vanguard with just $5 bil-
lion in revenue, 5 percent of Toyota's annual sales.
Dana's Morcott cites an Adrian, Michigan, company
called Brazeway, with only $70 million a year in rev-

Table 2.1 A Comparison of Vanguard Companies' Global Strategies.

Dana Corp.
Headquarters: Toledo, Ohio
Makes: automotive parts
Value $7.6 billion in revenue, 1996
Global strategy: to have 50% of revenue outside U.S. by 2000, through collection of company-owned plants and joint ventures

Toyota Motor Co.
Headquarters: Tokyo, Japan
Makes: automobiles, plus wide range of subsidiaries from banking to manufactured housing
Value: $100 million
Global strategy: Expand international sales through basic family of vehicles fine-tuned for individual markets, and produced locally.

Cummins Engine Co.
Headquarters: Columbus, Ind.
Makes: engines, industrial power equipment
Value: $5.5 billion
Global strategy: Expand in strategic markets through joint ventures, using Cummins-developed manufacturing, engineering and marketing processes.

ABB Asea Brown Bovera
Headquarters: Zurich, Switzerland
Makes: electrical-engineering equipment, such as robots and power plants
Value: $26 billion
Global strategy: has 1,300 indepedently incorporated subsidiaries, each ideally run by local managers

---

enue as another example of a global manufacturer. Brazeway makes heat evaporators used in frost-free freezers. At first glance, it might seem such a product might have limited appeal. In the United States, frost-free freezers have long been on sale. But in Europe, consumers used to chipping frost from the icebox on a weekly basis from aging refrigerators are only now replacing appliances made decades ago. And many consumers in Latin America and Asia don't even have home freezers, meaning ample opportunity for Brazeway to find a market as consumers buy new and improved products from its customers like Whirlpool, Maytag and Amana.

Even so, says Morcott, such small company global success stories are likely the exception rather than the global rule. "Clearly, financial strength is a given. Somebody without financial strength, well, the smaller companies are struggling because they can't concurrently grow operations in South America, Southeast Asia, Eastern Europe all at the same time. Critical mass is very important in the global arena. There's a certain critical mass you almost have to have to be meaningful," Morcott says.

"If you say, 'I want to be a global manufacturer of axles,' you'd better come to the table with a lot of money because you are in a high-stakes poker game. So, you can get to almost any kind of poker table on this global plane. You can play at a $2 limit table or you can play at a $1 million limit table. The stakes are endless," Morcott adds.

Cummins Chief Financial Officer Kirin Patel agrees. "In an industry like ours, an engine factory in India is a minimum of $100 million," he says. "That takes a lot of resources." Ford found that out the hard way. It linked up with Volkswagen in the late 1980s to form a venture in Brazil and Argentina called AutoLatina. Each company was trying to offset the seemingly insurmountable risk of operating in the two countries by sharing profits and losses 50–50. There were far more of the latter as the pair tried unsuccessfully to market products in countries where the inflation rate was 2,000 percent a month.

By 1995, the Brazilian and Argentine markets had stabilized, leading economists to predict the two countries could soon offer significant profit opportunities. But Volkswagen unexpectedly pulled out to go off on its own, leaving Ford to start from scratch. It lost nearly $1 billion in cleaning up the remains of AutoLatina and had to invest another $2.1 billion to jumpstart its own new ventures, including a new plant in southern Brazil announced in fall, 1997. Ford managed to earn money in Latin America in 1997, more than a decade after the company's first stab at the market and more than three years after the joint venture failed. But it expects a loss in 1998 due to economic uncertainty in the region.

Yet Vanguard members acknowledge staying out of the global fray may prove more costly in the long run than jumping in. At Dana, CFO Simpson explains the company aims for 10 percent annual sales growth, with about two-thirds coming from acquisitions and one-third from internal growth. Then it wants a 5 percent return on sales (often called a *profit margin*) across the board, 6 percent at each of its divisions (the 1 percent difference is to cover corporate expenditures). He sees global expansion as the only way Dana can meet those targets. "If you stay where you are, you aren't really going anywhere. You have to plow ahead," he says. "Let's assume we don't make any more acquisitions. We'd see cash flow like we've never seen in our lives. Our need for working capital would decrease, our need for acquisition money would decrease. But you risk a dilution of your capital base and a lack of growth." Says the Dana executive: "It's a productivity of the balance sheet, just as we talk about productivity of human capital."

Dana Europe President Gus Franklin adds that com-

panies must make that strong balance sheet work for
them at the local end. "You've got to be big to have the
strength to go globally but you've got to be small in the
way you approach each market and each customer,"
Franklin explains. "You've got to be big so that your
customers have faith in who you are, but when you
show up in Thailand, you've got to be able to act like a
small company, a small chain, acting with the local customers, the local buyers, the local infrastructure and
work together like heck."

Like Dana, Cummins in recent years has aligned its
operations to focus on its own core businesses, including diesel engines, automotive products, and industrial
power equipment. That, says Patel, has eliminated the
competition between operations in the United States
and elsewhere for financial resources. "It's not 'us' versus 'them.' We don't think in terms of a balance between domestic and international. We think of the market for a particular product, and then maybe we make
the investment that makes sense for that market."

For a Vanguard member with limited operations outside its home market, making the correct investments
is as delicate as cutting facets in a fine diamond. One
slip, and disaster can strike. That is why Chrysler CEO
Robert Eaton demands that the automaker's international ventures provide a higher rate of return than the
7.5 percent net margins that Chrysler has been earning
in North America during the 1990s. It is why Chrysler
is taking its time as other automakers race past it on
dusty developing country roads, searching for plant
sites. Says Eaton, "It's got to be a greater return over
time, than in this market, because the risk is higher. It
all comes down to individual decisions. You make the
decisions based on what you believe the return is going to be."

Those investment decisions are never easy, even for a company with the financial strength of Toyota. The Japanese automaker recognized in the early 1990s that pickup truck sales were on the verge of exploding in North America. U.S. executives pleaded with Japanese officials numerous times for funds to build a pickup truck plant. There was no question that Toyota could afford the project, but executives in Japan were hesitant to produce a vehicle that could be sold in only a handful of markets. The cries grew louder as truck sales climbed above 40 percent of the U.S. market. Finally, in 1995, Toyota chose a site outside Evansville, Indiana, where production is set to begin in 1998.

Toyota North American Manufacturing President Mikio "Mike" Kitano says Toyota's formidable balance sheet can be a hindrance in trying to expand. "It's a weakness," Kitano declared over dinner during the summer of 1997, surprising guests who had expected him to take the opposite view. He continued, "If all the people think we have the money, naturally they are going to be spoiled. If people always think we have money, they are not going to stretch themselves." However, Kitano says other companies' push into global markets has kept Toyota on its toes. "Competition is always good for a company. Without competition, people waste a company's resources."

Resources—People and Technology

Once a company has a global vision and the money to fund an international push, the final ingredient is implementation. To Dana's Morcott, that happens with only one tool. "You've got to have the people to do it. For $2 billion companies, or even $5 billion companies, that's where they hit the wall. It takes a lot of good people to do things," Morcott says.

Adds Alexander Doll Company Chairman Herb Brown, "People are the key, absolutely the key to the kingdom."

Toyota's Okuda agrees: "The most important ingredient [for a global manufacturer] is the quality of the people." This aspect is so important to Toyota that it takes precedence in every strategic decision concerning its global growth. Over the past decade, as Toyota searched around the world for sites to build new plants, it had one priority in mind. It was not location, because local governments had showered Toyota over the years with potential plant sites. Neither was it the size of incentive packages the company could expect, because any community would be happy to pay some of Toyota's costs. And Toyota did not worry whether its suppliers would be willing to set up shop nearby, because they had done so repeatedly. Toyota's key criterion was whether the community near the plant could provide potential employees who had the skills and teamwork attitude that working in a Toyota plant would require.

"It is the people," says Toyota Canada General Manager Andy Wantunabe, who headed Toyota's global plant site selection committee in the 1980s and early 1990s. Wantunabe personally reviewed every potential location, from wheat fields in Quebec to cow pastures in England. "We need population and knowledge. Those are very key to the organization."

Wantunabe's own background demonstrates how Toyota is making use of its managers' experience. He first caught Okuda's eye while he was in charge of the plant site selection committee. His work there won him the task of drafting Toyota's global business plan,

Okuda's "Great Leap Forward." Among Wantunabe's recommendations was that Toyota expand its Cambridge, Ontario, plant so that it could produce more Corollas and produce a Camry-derived car that could be sold in North American and around the world. Okuda was so taken with Wantunabe's insistence on Cambridge's potential that he placed him in charge of the expanded assembly plant—a key assignment for any Toyota manager who hopes to climb higher. Says Okuda, smiling, "By the time someone gets to the management level, we expect them to have a variety of experiences."

Such diversely trained employees, who have broken free of the assumptions that an engineer can only be an engineer, or a plant manager must stay a plant manager, have become a hallmark of Vanguard companies. These companies have also emphasized the importance of populating their ranks with managers from different backgrounds. Among top management at Cummins Engine, only CEO Henderson has not held an assignment outside the United States. President Theodore Solso ran Cummins's plant in Darlington, England, while CFO Patel, who was born in India, ran its Brazilian operations. "It's something that we talk about a lot and pay attention to, not simply because it's the right thing to do, but the right thing for our business," Patel says.

At Dana, international experience is required to gain one of the company's top 30 management jobs, along with experience in three of six other specialties, such as finance, manufacturing, or marketing. But even those employees who won't work abroad are encouraged through the Dana Style to take part in company affairs, set their own standards and performance measurements, and take 40 hours of classes each year. As

Dana's philosophy states, "People are our most important asset."

ABB, under Barnevik, may have won honors for the most diverse collection of executives and managers. Barnevik repeatedly hammered on his managers the need to always look outside. During his tenure at the company, ABB's eight-member executive committee was made up of German, Swedish, U.S., Swiss, and Danish officials. Its 150-member headquarters staff boasted people from 20 countries. Barnevik sent out 500 young managers at a time around the globe, searching for new markets, new methods, and new opportunities. Then he brought them home to one of ABB's 1,400 different businesses to make sure his global gospel percolated through the organization. To make sure that no culture became dominant, Barnevik declared that English would be ABB's common language and that its financial statements would be denoted in U.S. dollars, because both have become accepted worldwide as common ground standards. After all, even communist Cuba officially does business in dollars.

"When after some years they return home . . . they will have learned that their own culture is not always the measure for all things," Barnevik says. At the end of the day, he admits, "all people are 'local,' with their roots in some home country. It therefore takes a major, systematic, and sustained effort to bridge the borders, build the multinational teams," and create a global enterprise. But, Barnevik says, "it is well worthwhile." He has not abandoned these practices at his new company. Barnevik left ABB in 1997 to run Sweden's Investor from London, a shock to Sweden's business community, which mourned the relocation of a premier company.

"Percy is a person with a vision that works," says

management professor Manfred Kets de Vries. "He knows a great deal about how to motivate people."

Yet Barnevik himself is the first to downplay the significance of vision in and of itself. There are enough people with bright ideas in the world, he declares: "In business, success is 5 percent strategy, 95 percent execution."[4]

Making a global enterprise much easier to build than it would have been even five years ago is the rapid spread of information technology (IT). The use of computers, linked by worldwide communications systems, has led to the creation of companies that can operate virtually 24 hours a day. General Motors International President Louis Hughes says the advantage of having his office in Zurich is that he can communicate with GM's Asian operations in the morning, before employees leave for home at the end of the work day in places like Tokyo and Beijing, and then talk with colleagues in Detroit and São Paulo in the afternoon as they are arriving for work at the start of their day. With an electronic mail system like Lotus Notes, managers can send information to one another no matter what time zone they are in. Video conferences make it easy to link managers sitting on either side of an ocean.

Declares Barnevik, "The writing is on the wall: Globalization of business demands global organization. You can't do that without it [information technology].[5] At ABB, Barnevik boasted 50,000 PCs and 45,000 e-mail users: "If you don't have an understanding of speed in the world and the impact of IT on business, you are going to be a loser." Yet information technology, and indeed, any type of manufacturing or engineering technology, is not the answer in itself. Vanguard companies have discovered that these tools are only as useful as the people who are making use of them.

Early in the 1990s, manufacturers around the world had turned to robots and other types of automation in a bid to improve their quality and cut their labor rates. It became standard practice to marshall groups of school children and visiting dignitaries down assembly lines, where they'd gaze in awe as robots would perform tasks such as welding or selecting parts for circuit boards. GM even had an experimental "Factory of the Future" in Saginaw, Michigan, where virtually all the plant manager had to do was flick a switch each day.

But as the 1990s come to a close, industry has come to the realization that robots alone are not the answer, and neither will automation guarantee a global manufacturer's success. For one thing, robots are expensive—millions of dollars apiece—meaning it takes years to amortize the cost. For another, they are only capable of being programmed to perform one task at a time, unlike humans, who are able to switch from one job to another as production requires. By 1997, says Chrysler Advanced Manufacturing Vice President Frank Ewasyshyn, robots had simply become another manufacturing tool. "Buying a robot today is like buying a toaster—you take it home, you plug it in, and it works. The expectation level is so high, robots are commodity buys. They're nothing special."

What is special, Ewasyshyn says, is the way technology has helped manufacturers communicate better with their suppliers and their customers. Chrysler requires that its suppliers use the same Catia software that Chrysler has at its design studios and computer labs. Catia, designed by France's Dassault Systemes, provides a three-dimensional view of every step in the product design process, from a car's outward appearance to individual parts. The view is translated into a mathematical calculation that provides the specifications needed to order a part or make changes. Catia has become so advanced that Chrysler can set up a section of the assembly line where the part will be needed and simulate how the part might be attached to the car, changing the part's specifications and the assembly process on a single computer screen. Says Ewasyshyn, "There will always be problems, but communication is much better today. It helps if you clearly define your expectations."

"In the past, maybe we've been too impatient looking for quick fixes," acknowledges GM's Eric Stephens. "We looked for the major solution and missed that fact that the answers are all in simple, little things."

As Vanguard companies build plants around the world, they are learning to take advantage of local conditions. Factories in low labor-rate countries like Mexico, Thailand, and Brazil feature much less automation, like welding robots and stamping presses, than industry pundits had forecast they would have even a few years ago. The reason is simple: When companies are paying employees just a few dollars a day, there is no need to install expensive equipment whose cost will take years to recoup. People can simply do the jobs themselves for much less money, even over the long run. At Mercedes-Benz's new factory in Tuscaloosa, Alabama, only 25 percent of the work is automated. Mercedes is striving to see what its new, inexperienced workforce is capable of doing. If it were to install too much automation, it might never get a handle on the types of tasks workers can or cannot perform. Companies that think globalization is merely an opportunity to put cookie-cutter plants in spots around the world need to reevaluate those expectations: All they may end up with is the same set of problems spread from one end of the globe to another. After all, GM's factory of the future is now a thing of the past. It closed, without fanfare, in the mid-1990s.

Dana's Morcott, for one, says the ultimate balance between strategy, strength, people, and technology, must come from within.

"We never suggest to anyone that you try and duplicate a Dana, or that you benchmark or role model us," he says. "Frankly, I don't care if anybody copies us. We don't have enough staff or anything. If you say, 'here's something that works for this company and maybe we can evolve toward that direction and find our own sort of legs as we go,' fine. But to just try to take our charts and fill in your names, it isn't going to work."

Dana's strategy was devised based on a 100-year history that had already included an emphasis on international operations. Says Morcott, "You shouldn't touch any organization if you don't understand the culture and the heritage and the history of that organization. If you start fiddling with an organization, as people are doing today in spades, without considering tradition, culture, and history, I think you're setting yourself up for a big surprise."

He continues, "It isn't that you can't change these things, you can. But if you're not considering the importance of that, watch out. You can consider its importance and still do it, but at least you've weighed in the human psyche and what it means to play around with what people hold near and dear."

3

The One Essential Tool

There is no magic formula to ensure global manufacturing success. But one essential tool is necessary to attempt it: a manufacturing process.

Sometimes called a "production system," or an "operating system," a manufacturing process is most commonly defined as a set of standards that governs the way a product is produced within the four walls of a factory. But at Vanguard companies, the manufacturing process is as much a statement of philosophy as a series of production controls. It is not something left to "the manufacturing guys" to implement, rather it is a tool that has applications for all. A Vanguard company's manufacturing process can be explained in a few sentences, elaborated upon in an afternoon.

At these companies, global success has come largely

because the manufacturing systems have been applied, embraced, and understood. They incorporate both a set of values and a system of practical guidelines. The manufacturing process provides the backbone of everything that touches manufacturing, from product development to customer delivery. It is a consistent message to employees, management, and customers of what the company wishes to stand for. "We knew what best practices were, but we wanted to put best practices into words," says Cummins Engine CEO James Henderson.

Above all, a manufacturing process is the way a company leverages the skills of all its employees says Chrysler Executive Vice President Dennis Pawley. "A bad process—or no process—will destroy a great person every time," Pawley says.

The Toyota Production System

One manufacturing process stands above all the others: the Toyota Production System (TPS). It is the most studied, imitated, and revered system in global manufacturing. "Nobody has a production system that is in the same universe as Toyota," says James Womack, coauthor of *The Machine That Changed the World,* a book that opened the manufacturing world's eyes to the efficiency of Toyota's production methods. The first stop for any company that is devising its own manufacturing system must be Toyota. In the United States, interest in TPS is so great that Toyota set up a Supplier Support Center (misnamed, since its participants range far beyond Toyota's supply base) to teach TPS to those who are interested. TPS has provided the foundation that has enabled Toyota to build its global market.

The fundamental principle is shockingly simple: TPS is designed to serve customers' needs by eliminating waste in all parts of the organization. Waste can be driven out of production time, from reducing workers' motions and line-side inventory levels to speeding up product delivery. As a result of eliminating waste, quality rises, workers feel fulfilled, customers are satisfied, and a company prospers.[1] "TPS is like a vast conveyor that starts with customer orders and culminates in deliveries of finished products," Toyota says.

TPS has its roots in the creation of Toyota as a maker of weaving looms in 1902. Company founder Sakichi Toyoda ("da" is correct: the family changed the company's ending to "ta" so it would be easier to pronounce) invented an automatic loom that would instantly shut down if any of the threads being woven snapped. Later, Toyota would name this automatic shutdown system *jidoka* and it would become a key ingredient of the company's success. When Toyota turned to automobile manufacturing in 1936, Sakichi's son, Kiichiro, traveled to Dearborn, Michigan, to observe Henry Ford's factories. He saw that Ford had divided auto production into three elements: the conveyor belt, which moved parts and car bodies down the assembly line; a division of labor, in which workers handled just one step of the production process; and parts inventory flow, in which the components needed for the job were stacked behind workers or stored in areas of the factory.

Kiichiro Toyoda knew that the small production volumes in Japan couldn't support massive operations, like the Rouge complex, that Ford had built in the United States. So he concentrated on ways Toyota could adapt Ford's ideas to its own lower volumes. His breakthrough concept was an idea called "just-in-time" delivery, which has become his lasting legacy. Kiichiro Toyoda streamlined inventories throughout Toyota's factories, so that workers had only the materials they needed when they needed them. Working with Toyota's company-owned suppliers and independent parts producers, Kiichiro Toyoda arranged for deliveries to be made frequently, and in small lots. That freed up space inside Toyota's factories where parts would normally be stored. It required Toyota to share production information with its suppliers, and to be in close communication with its dealers, so that the company built vehicles it could sell quickly. This was the beginning of what Toyota would later name the "pull" system. It does not build vehicles until it has orders for them or until it sees consistent market demand.

World War II interrupted the fledgling steps Toyota was taking in auto manufacturing. Its factories were given over to armament production, and many were damaged by Allied bombs. Toyota's need to rebuild after the war provided the opportunity for the formal creation of TPS. The system's acknowledged father, Taiichi Ohno, has become an almost godlike figure in manufacturing circles. Says Chrysler's Pawley, "When I die, I hope they put on my tombstone, 'He was Chrysler's Dr. Ohno.' " The reverence paid to Ohno amuses some of the engineers who collaborated with him from the 1940s until his death in 1992. They knew Ohno as a contradictory taskmaster with little time for inefficiency and muddled thinking. "It was not always pleasant. He was always yelling at us," recalls Chihiro Nakao, President of Shin-Gijutsu Company, who spent 30 years working with Ohno at Toyota. Yet Ohno's legendary bursts of temper quickly subsided, recalls Nakao, who himself has been labeled a *sensei* (master) for his deep understanding of manufacturing. "Mr.

Ohno fired me seven times at Toyota, but eight times I was welcomed back into the clan."

Ohno's work began in a Toyota machine shop. He watched as workers struggled to complete their tasks and decided that jobs might be performed more quickly if the work was completed in the order in which it needed to be done. Ohno attempted to keep parts moving in one direction—a concept that would later be called "continuous flow," a key part of TPS.

Ohno's real inspiration came from a trip to the United States in 1946. Like Kiichiro Toyoda, he spent time visiting Ford's factories. But he was far more fascinated by trips to American supermarkets, which dwarfed the tiny "mom and pop" food stores that are still prevalent in Japan. At the supermarkets, Ohno saw that customers chose exactly what they wanted, in the quantities they desired, and shopped according to the pace that they set for themselves. As supermarket shelves emptied, they were restocked, often from the rear, allowing merchandise to constantly be pushed forward within consumers' reach. He saw that the supermarkets did not keep huge stocks of corn flakes or cartons of milk piled up in back; they relied on constant deliveries from vendors so that products would stay fresh.

From his observations, Ohno built on the fundamentals of just-in-time delivery and the pull system to create what would ultimately become TPS. In order to understand the system, Ohno said companies had to accept three basic conditions: (1) Top management had to make a strong commitment to the system, participate directly in implementing it, and reinforce its principles with middle management; (2) all employees, from the shop floor to plant offices, had to participate; and (3) everyone, managers, workers, and suppliers,

---

Table 3.1 Three Conditions for Embracing TPS.

• Management commitment
• Employee participation
• Training and reeducation

Source: Toyota

---

needed constant training and updating in what the system required. Says Nakao, "The biggest issue is the leadership of top management. If they are not willing to lead the entire fight, the whole battle is over."

Under TPS, every Toyota factory is run on common principles. First, they focus on customers' needs, using just-in-time inventory as their main method to accomplish this. Ohno's insistence on this led to the creation of a system called "kanban." Kanbans themselves are plastic cards, stamped with bar codes, that accompany every basket and rack of parts delivered to the assembly line. Even engines have their own kanban cards. When the parts supplies run low, a worker pulls the kanban card out of the basket or off the end of a rack of parts and puts it into a bin. A materials handler makes frequent sweeps down the assembly line to pick up cards and restock the necessary parts.

In accordance with just-in-time delivery, Ohno decreed plants would run on a system of "leveled production." He admitted it was simpler for workers and factories simply to build large quantities, or batches, of vehicles, based on Toyota's assumption that its dealers could eventually sell them. But workers who weren't needed to build a certain type of vehicle might stand idly by. And dealers might be stuck waiting for one or two vehicles that hadn't been produced. If the vehicles didn't arrive, customers might walk away. So instead of batch production, Toyota plants build a variety of vehicles or products throughout the day, in an effort to precisely match dealers' orders. Leveling production allows Toyota to keep its workforce busy and keep vehicles flowing more evenly to dealers.

Ohno devised a way to measure how much time each worker would need to carry out his or her tasks in this customer-driven pull system. The measurement is called *"takt* time," from the German word for the musical count that is ticked off by a metronome. Simply put, *takt* time is measured by dividing the number of vehicles that must be produced that hour by 60 minutes. If 60 vehicles must be built, one vehicle must be completed every 60 seconds, which means a 60-second *takt* time. Toyota also calculates the *takt* time for every individual process in the plant, leading up to the moment that a car is driven off the assembly line. It is able to do so because of one of TPS's other key principles: standardized work.

Every work station in a Toyota plant, some 600 in all, has a standardized work chart. Each chart shows how Toyota has broken down the movements, tools, and parts that are required to perform that function. By placing the charts in sequence, it is possible to follow on paper the steps it takes to build a car, from assembling the first parts to the final production at the end of the assembly line. Each worker is expected to follow the prescribed production process, to the letter, every time a car body reaches his or her work station. However, the processes are not set in stone for perpetuity. Toyota encourages workers to offer continual suggestions for improving how the task can be performed.

Employee ideas and feedback for improving work efficiency is a process called *kaizen,* and it is a key func-

---

Table 3.2 Guiding Principles of TPS.

I. Just-in-time production
   a. Customer focus
   b. Leveled production
   c. Pull system
   d. Continuous flow
   e. Takt time
   f. Multi-skilled workers
II. *Jidoka*
III. Standardized work
IV. *Kaizen*

Source: Toyota

---

tion of every person in the Toyota system. Almost daily in some plants, certainly weekly in all, Toyota work teams, comprising about 10 to 15 people, meet to discuss how their jobs can be improved, both to increase the quality of the vehicles being built and to raise employee comfort and safety levels. Since each work team is responsible for the tasks that are performed in its section of the assembly line, workers are trained to handle multiple tasks. They frequently switch jobs during an eight-hour shift to relieve monotony and to give Toyota an optimum number of people familiar with each production process. As a result, all suggestions on process improvements are thoroughly discussed because each team member may end up performing the task at hand.

Chrysler's Pawley says this problem-solving process is the single most contributing factor in Toyota's success. "Everybody in the outside world thinks they are perfect, but they would be the first to tell you they're not perfect," Pawley says. "They have just as many problems as anybody else. The difference is, they know they are going to have problems, but they have a model by which they solve problems faster."

Toyota acknowledges that the *kaizen* system can lead to pressure on its assembly line workers. So the company developed two release valves. One is the *jidoka* system, originated by the company's founder. Throughout a Toyota assembly plant, machinery is designed on a fail-safe basis. Should a part be inserted incorrectly, if a hole in a metal fixture is not drilled properly, or if a worker fails to tighten a bolt to the proper degree, the machinery shuts down. This prevents defective parts or cars from proceeding down the assembly line. Generally, a *jidoka* will trigger an instant response from a team leader or engineer assigned to patrol the area. The error must be corrected before the machine is restarted.

There is a second, manual method to accomplish the same goal: the *andon,* a device intended to stop the assembly line. An *andon* is most often a yellow cord hanging above the line, or a button posted at each work station. Every employee, from factory floor to management, is authorized to pull the *andon* cord if a problem occurs.

There is a mistaken impression among those who have never actually seen an *andon* that a pull on the cord will immediately cause a production line to screech to a dead stop. That's not the case at Toyota. A single pull on an *andon* cord merely signals a problem. Generally, this illuminates a light on a tracking board overhead, called an *andon* board, that shows the identification number of the work station where the trouble has occurred. When they see the light, other workers or team leaders quickly come to investigate. But the line does not shut down unless there is a second tug on the *andon* cord. Vehicle bodies remain in motion through one more work station, allowing time for workers who are not affected by the problem to finish their tasks.

The value of TPS for other companies is often as misunderstood as the *andon*. A company with a less workerfriendly culture, or that does not communicate well with suppliers and vendors, may fail to realize the benefits of the system, Toyota says. "It only works when companies invest the system with the dynamism of human creativity and initiative. TPS works because it gives people a chance to become as good as they can be," the automaker adds. "Everyone has a role to play. But they must begin by trusting each other."

Toyota officials say this trust has been the key to TPS's success in its plants around the world. Toyota North American President Mikio "Mike" Kitano is skeptical of companies that head out to become global players without a set of manufacturing principles.

"That is a kind of arrogance," says Kitano, who managed Toyota's California joint venture with General Motors (GM), New United Motor Manufacturing Inc., as well as Toyota's plant in Motomachi, Japan. "Some companies are very focused on strategy. They say, 'We can grow globally wide.' But, I'm afraid of that kind of globalization . . . What does it mean?" asks the bearded executive.

THE CUMMINS PRODUCTION SYSTEM

Globalization wasn't even being discussed at Cummins Engine when officials set off in 1988 to create the Cummins Production System. But the Columbus, Indiana, company was feeling intense heat from international competition. Throughout the 1980s, it was feeling pressure from Japanese engine manufacturers such as Hino and Komatsu, which were taking dead aim at Cummins's dozen major customers. Cummins had fought back with a vengeance, hiring quality consultants to improve its products, establishing benchmarks based on production at other companies to see how it could streamline its factories, launching a 30-month quality blitz, slashing its own prices 30 percent to keep a grip on the business its rivals were trying to steal, and announcing major investments in new families of more efficient engines.

Just as the new engine programs were getting off the ground, Cummins faced a potentially life-threatening blow. Japanese companies cut their prices 30 percent below the levels where Cummins had trimmed its prices. Meanwhile, test results on the new engine families showed that as the engines aged, they would produce too much soot, violating federal emissions standards. Clearly, Cummins faced a dilemma. It had to reduce its costs dramatically so that it could match Japanese companies' prices and maintain its profit margins. And it had to dramatically improve the long-term quality of its engines or face losing even the customers that it might otherwise retain. "We said, 'God, what's going on here?'" says Cummins Executive Vice President Joseph Loughrey.

The solution became the Cummins Production System (CPS). Fostered as a response to a crisis, it has since been implemented in Cummins's 40 plants around the world. It has been studied by companies as diverse as Boeing, IVECO, and Robert Bosch and it is now taught in eight languages, including Portuguese and Maranthi. Work began in late 1988, when a team of Cummins executives, including then-President Henderson, swept out across the United States and to Cummins's overseas plants, looking to see if they could find any solutions to the company's problems within its own ranks.

"The simple conclusion that we came to was that we had islands of excellence. We saw people at different places doing truly wonderful things, very consistent with what we were hoping for," Loughrey says. "But they were islands, unconnected. There was no systemic approach. There were people reinventing the wheel, starting all over when somebody had figured out how do to it someplace else. We said, 'We've got to change that.' "

The benchmark work began again in earnest. Teams were dispatched to study production systems at Toyota and camera maker Canon. Loughrey (pronounced low-cree) traveled to Japan to visit competitor Hino, where the contrast between Cummins and its rival was stark. At Cummins's main engine plant in Columbus, it was not uncommon for dozens of completed engines to sit in stacks at the end of an assembly line, waiting to be tested, waiting for repairs, or waiting for customer orders. At Hino, "We watched the engines come off the line and boom! Here came the guy with the forklift, and off they went to the test area or off to a truck. I never saw more than three engines sitting in the holding area. And we had a thousand or two thousand," Loughrey says.

By June, Loughrey's team had written a "white paper" outlining the fundamentals of what they felt the system should have. Gathering in a conference room above the Cummins headquarters cafeteria, team members summoned managers from the company's 10 largest plants, plus senior manufacturing officials. Over the next several days, the managers debated the fundamental beliefs behind the system. "We were trying to create a framework, like the skeleton of a person, that hangs together and interacts well," says Loughrey.

"Now, how do we involve the maximum number of people, like muscles, and build on it?" The group settled on the phrase "Customer-led quality" and decided that CPS should focus on a comprehensive set of standards for operating each of Cummins's 40 factories.

CPS's goal, Loughrey explained, was to enable each Cummins plant to become the industry's best in the eyes of its customers, whether it was a parts plant that supplied other Cummins factories, or a Cummins plant shipping engines to a major customer. And, CPS hopefully would lead to continuous improvement throughout Cummins's factories by standardizing four major areas: common practices, common functions, common training, and common measures.

In the years since Cummins implemented CPS, GM and other companies have seized upon the word "common" to refer to cookie cutter processes, like painting and body shop functions, that they want all their plants to achieve. But, says Loughrey, "We used the word common because we want people to do things similarly, not necessarily exactly."

CPS involved 10 basic practices. The first two, "Putting the Customer First" and "Synchronize Flows," were aimed at making sure Cummins's workers knew what their role was. Like Toyota, Cummins wanted its plants to be driven by a pull system, based on customers' desires. Like Toyota, it wanted components to move in one direction, toward the customer, as they made their journey down the assembly line, and it wanted workers to arrange their jobs so that there were no backward steps in the production process.

The third and fourth principles, "Build Quality In" and "Involve People Through Teams," were aimed at the plant's management team, which, Loughrey says, is responsible for making sure workers have an intellectual understanding of the importance of quality products, and the training so that they can implement improvements. The fifth and six principles, "Ensure Equipment Is Available and Capable" and "Create Functional Excellence," are aimed at maintenance workers, both those assigned to maintenance jobs and those assembly line workers responsible for keeping their work stations clean and in good repair. The seventh principle, "Establish the Right Environment" is fundamental to workers being able to easily perform their jobs. Factories need to be simply laid out, with many visual systems such as *andon* boards that make it easy to spot problems. "I want anybody to be able to walk into a plant and to get a sense of what's going on in the plant," Loughrey says.

The eighth principle, "Treat Suppliers as Partners" applies to both the plant floor and to Cummins's relationship with the outside world. Loughrey says Cummins considers its suppliers to include local schools, which are training students who could eventually take jobs at Cummins's operations. He's particularly concerned that students aren't learning the math skills that will enable them to solve problems in the assembly line. The ninth principle, "Follow the Seven Steps for Problem Solving," offers a seven-step program for problem solving, to be used by workers throughout the company. Every employee at Cummins, from the factory floor to company offices, receives a pocket-sized card with the seven steps printed on them. The steps include finding the problem, figuring out possible causes, finding a solution, testing the solution to see if it works, and eventually improving upon the solution. The seven steps lead to the tenth and final principle, "Follow the Continuous Improvement Process."

To implement the 10 steps of CPS, the team chose

three Cummins plants and came up with the phrase "Top down, bottom up and communicate like hell" to summarize expectations of how CPS would be carried out. Each plant was assigned a pilot project that would fulfill each expectation. For top-down, each plant was expected to implement a change throughout the factory, such as the presentation of parts to the assembly line. For bottom-up, each plant took a section of the assembly line and implemented the CPS principles throughout that section. "Communicate like hell" meant sharing the CPS principles and results of the projects not only in the selected plants, but between the plants and with other plants not yet affected by the project. Even as they were assigning the CPS projects to the three pilot plants, Loughrey's team ran into resistance from managers frazzled and fed up with years of different attempts to fix the company's problems. "We were asked very directly, 'Why shouldn't we think of this as the program of the month?' " Loughrey says. "My answer was very simple: 'Five years from now, I'm still going to be involved in this. Number two,

---

Table 3.3 The Cummins Production System.

---

1. *Put* the customer first
2. Synchronize flows
3. Build quality in
4. Involve people through teams
5. Ensure equipment is available and capable
6. Create functional excellence
7. Establish the right environment
8. Treat suppliers as partners
9. Use seven steps for problem solving
10. Follow the continuous improvement process

Source: Cummins

---

we're going to get so good at this that we're going to have a worldwide convention to show each other what we've done.' I got a lot of guffaws."

CPS was swiftly implemented despite plant managers' reservations. The first year, the pilot programs spread from three plants to 10. By the end of 1992, programs had been implemented in all Cummins factories, including its newly reopened Cummins Mid-Range Engine Plant (CMEP), which had been closed the previous three years due to business lost to Cummins's Japanese competition. CMEP became the first Cummins plant to implement CPS across its operations and to use a team-based work system that Loughrey felt would best reflect the CPS principles. Meanwhile, Loughrey and his team made frequent sweeps of Cummins's plants—an average of more than 150 a year—to measure the progress they were making to implement the system. "We had to do a lot of things to reinforce the program," Loughrey says.

Once the system had spread companywide, Cummins saw that it was clearly paying off. Since 1991, Cummins has posted double digit improvements in everything from inventory turns to reducing delivery time. But Loughrey isn't satisfied. "If you divide these numbers by six years, it's not fast enough," the executive says. Cummins is diving even deeper into CPS so that its plants can understand where they stand relative to each other and learn from improvements each has made. In 1994, the company instituted the Cummins Production Excellence System (CPES, pronounced "seeps"), a series of measurements of plant performance, devised by company managers. Each plant grades itself in eight areas, including leadership, shop operations, materials handling, quality, manufacturing, engineering, finance, and human resources.

Then the plant managers give their factories scores on each of the 10 CPS fundamentals. Below 50 percent proficiency is a "minus;" 50 percent to 69 percent proficiency is a I; 70 percent to 84 percent proficiency is a II; 85 percent to 94 percent proficiency is a III; and above 94 percent proficiency wins a CPE designation. Scores on all 18 criteria are totaled to come up with a final rating, but no plant's overall score can exceed its worst rating. Thus, a I in one area results in a I for the plant—even if it gets IIIs or even CPEs in all other areas.

The plant managers are very tough on themselves. In late 1997, a CPES chart for Cummins's 40 plants showed only two plant managers awarded their factories top CPE ratings in any of the eight categories. A number of the plant managers gave themselves "minuses" and most plants' overall ratings were Is or IIs. No plant has yet gotten a III as its overall rating; once one does, Cummins plans to send in an audit team to double-check the plant manager's assessment. "It's a way for people to talk to one another about how they're doing and what their issues are," Loughrey says of CPES.

Table 3.4 Improvements through CPS, 1991 to 1997.

Inventory turns	Up 56%
Defects	Down 52%
Scrap	Down 71%
Lead time	Down 74%
Safety violations	Down 52%
Throughput	Up 39%
Productivity	Up 35%
Delivery time	Down 17%

Source: Cummins

He admits the results can be embarrassing, since each plant manager gets the score sheet for all plants. "Everybody knows. But it gets people to ask, 'How come we got that score?' Or, 'What did they do to get so good?' "

Loughrey says CPS has been "extremely valuable" as Cummins has moved toward becoming a global company. The system is used in every country where Cummins operates. "It's all the same structure, the same goal, the same approach, the same training." When Cummins was negotiating its joint venture in India with Telco, Cummins specifically requested that CPS be used to operate the plant. "Because it's a skeleton, there's lots of room for innovation. You're not shoving something on somebody that's so rule-booky that they say, 'No way,' " Loughrey says.

Loughrey thinks CPS undoubtedly has helped Cummins become a better company. Since CPS's creation, Cummins has developed similar technical, engineering, and marketing processes as well as an umbrella system so that employees can see how they all fit together. Says Loughrey: "This is a learning process. We've learned tremendously about ourselves. We are finding out what do we do well, what do we need to do better? You learn to work with people that you trust. This way, there are a whole bunch of us that are all over this stuff, just trying to drive it home and understand it and learn ourselves."

THE CHRYSLER OPERATING SYSTEM

Unlike Cummins, which was thrust into creating its production system by a monumental crisis, Chrysler's financial troubles were well behind it when manufacturing chief Dennis Pawley first suggested the idea of an operating system to CEO Robert Eaton in 1994. Indeed, Chrysler's net income and profit margins were soaring, thanks to vehicles like the sexy Dodge Viper sports car, the sleek LH midsize sedans, and the Jeep Grand Cherokee. Landing on the covers of countless auto enthusiast magazines, these hot products had all but banished Chrysler's image of the 1980s as a producer of tinny, boxy K-cars. The transformation had come, in large part, because of the company's reorganization of its designers, engineers, and marketing and manufacturing experts into "platform teams" that each focused on one size of vehicle, such as small cars, large cars, minivans, or Jeeps. The streamlining had sliced the time Chrysler needed to develop a vehicle to less than three years, clearly the U.S. auto industry's best, and it had allowed the company to spend hundreds of millions of dollars fewer on product development that even its Japanese rivals.

But the shiny sheet metal and savings in time and money could not camouflage Chrysler's continued problems with quality. It consistently racked up substandard scores on customer surveys conducted by marketing experts J. D. Power and Associates, which measured defects soon after buyers purchased their vehicles and during the years they owned them. "It's too bad that the people who buy those cars . . . have as much trouble as they do," says Robert Knoll, former head of automotive testing at *Consumer Reports*. The company constantly found itself battling with government regulators over alleged defects in cars across its lineup, especially in its bread-and-butter minivans. To ensure the automaker's long-term viability, something had to be done.

Eaton called his executive team together in the summer of 1994 for a brainstorming session. The Colorado-born Eaton had left GM's European operations two years earlier to succeed celebrity CEO Lee Iacocca, the marketing wizard given credit for twice rescuing the number 3 U.S. auto company from bankruptcy. Eaton's timing was spectacular: He quit GM just a week before its board, angry at CEO Robert Stempel's procrastination in developing a comeback strategy, booted Stempel's management team and installed Eaton's former boss, international chief Jack Smith, as president. Eaton saw the potential that Chrysler offered to excel in the U.S. market. But, he told his executives at the 1994 gathering, he wanted Chrysler to look beyond North America. He wanted it to become the world's top automotive company and he wanted to make it happen by the year 2000.

Pawley quickly spoke up. Without an emphasis on manufacturing, he told Eaton and his fellow executives, Chrysler could not climb past standouts like Toyota, Mercedes, and BMW. Pawley's determination to raise the status of manufacturing has been a trademark throughout his career. After 22 years at GM, he suddenly took flight, jumping first to Japanese automaker Mazda, then to parts supplier United Technologies, and ultimately landing at Chrysler in 1990, two years before Eaton arrived. Throughout those years, he had suffered the slings and arrows of disrespect for his profession. Engineers, designers, and finance staff were the real power players when Pawley was climbing the corporate ladder. Manufacturing experts were misfits, left out of the process of creating a new car until just weeks before production was to begin. "All we had to do was beat 'em, heat 'em and ship 'em," he is fond of saying.

Yet even Detroit automakers grudgingly acknowledged that Toyota owed its exemplary success to its emphasis on manufacturing. And Pawley was emphatic that Chrysler's own success should stem from the same focus. He proposed to Eaton and his fellow executives that Chrysler shift its attention from the quick development of cars and trucks to a recognition of the importance of manufacturing. "This is where it happens. This is where Chrysler will live or die," Pawley says. "World-class companies are driven by manufacturing." Pawley wanted Chrysler to embrace the manufacturing world's equivalent of the platform teams—an operating system that would serve as a set of principles that guided every step the company took in the development and manufacturing process. Pawley called his plan the Chrysler Operating System, deliberately avoiding the words "production system." He sought to stress his system's application beyond the four walls of a factory, using a vivid analogy to prove his point. "If (Toyota CEO) Hiroshi Okuda and the half-dozen top executives from Toyota were on a plane coming over to benchmark Chrysler and the plane took a deep dive over the Pacific, what would happen? They'd probably have a service in a Shinto shrine somewhere. The next day the company would take off running just like it did the day before. I firmly believe that," Pawley

---

Table 3.5 Principles of the Chrysler Operating System.

---

1. Consistent production schedules
2. Consistent production methods across plants
3. Drive out waste
4. Training and education so worker morale remains high

Source: Chrysler

---

says.[2] (Former Toyota executive Nakao agrees: "When Mr. Ohno died, I just found myself following his path.")

But if a plane carrying Chrysler's team went down, Pawley says, "What would happen to this company? I think the son-of-a-bitch would dissolve."

Though trained as an engineer, Eaton had held deep respect for the craft of manufacturing since his first job in the 1950s at a GM axle plant at Mound and Nine Mile Roads in suburban Detroit. Manufacturing is "where the rubber meets the road," Eaton says. He needed no convincing by Pawley: "Clearly, we had to make big gains. And our answer is COS," says the CEO. Pawley set off with a team of four dozen manufacturing specialists, some drawn from the Massachusetts Institute of Technology's Leaders for Manufacturing program. Over 18 months, they visited Toyota, Cummins, and nearly 200 other companies, from Nike to Yoplait, seeing how they developed and produced products. "I don't care if you make widget or ice cream, there's something to be learned," Pawley says. Team members traveled to Japan and to Mexico, to Europe and to Latin America, getting to the point where they could recognize within 30 seconds if a factory was well run. They talked to experts like Loughrey and Nakao, trying to find out what was involved in embracing a manufacturing system.

Out of the visits came agreement on four key priorities for COS, starting with a focus on level production schedules. Fraught with cyclical patterns, automakers around the world had traditionally boosted plants' production with overtime when sales were hot, then sliced production through layoffs and shutdowns when sales cooled. The practice stemmed from their long-held view of labor as a variable cost that could be adjusted as sales dictated. But in the United States by the 1990s, United Auto Workers' contracts called for their members to be paid 95 percent of their pay and benefits even when their plants were not working. The guarantee was intended to prevent automakers from shutting down their factories at will, throwing workers out onto the street. In practice, the companies still relied on layoffs, despite the expense. Pawley saw the folly in paying workers for jobs they were not performing.

He also knew that smoothed production schedules would improve the quality of Chrysler's vehicles. Manufacturing experts have long known that machinery is at its optimum performance when it is in constant and high volume use, and least effective when production is continually jerking into motion or grinding to a stop. Smoothing schedules would provide a constant pace of production. That would put Chrysler in good stead with its suppliers, like Cummins, whose own operations suffered any time production was interrupted. And it would please dealers, who would not be frustrated waiting for vehicles to arrive. But to smooth production, Chrysler had to communicate closely with suppliers to ensure frequent parts deliveries, and with dealers so that it did not build vehicles that it could not sell.

Suppliers played a key role in COS's second priority: streamlining factories and instituting consistent production practices. Chrysler relies on parts makers for 75 percent of the components used on its cars. As Chrysler was changing the pace and processes inside its plants, so, too, did its suppliers need to adjust their own schedules and production methods. As a result, Chrysler began inviting suppliers to take part in the development process far earlier than they ever had before. As Pawley was drafting COS in 1994 and 1995,

Chrysler was beginning work on its next-generation LH sedans: Dodge Intrepid, Chrysler Concorde, and Eagle Vision. Instead of delivering parts specifications to suppliers after it had done its own development work, Chrysler's suppliers were invited into the project from the first day, as were the company's manufacturing specialists.

Everyone on the project used the same development software, Catia, produced by France's Dassault Systemes, so they could all communicate in the same computer language. The steps needed to produce the cars on the factory floor were first developed on computer screens, using parts that were created virtually by suppliers using the same system. Chrysler estimated the combination of Catia and COS saved it eight months of development time and $80 million over what might have been needed otherwise.

The savings exemplified COS's third priority: driving out waste. Pawley wanted his plants to reexamine every step they took to build a car, from the way parts were delivered to the assembly line to the tests that were conducted when the vehicles were being prepared for delivery. At its St. Louis, Missouri, minivan plant, Chrysler added teams of autoworker who acted as customer inspectors. They combed over each finished minivan, looking for defects that customers most frequently complained about, like water leaks, wind noise, and loose carpeting. If they discovered a problem, the inspectors were able to head straight for the assembly line to diagnose the changes that would be needed to correct it. This lowered the risk of Chrysler shipping a defective vehicle to a customers who might become disgruntled.

The inspectors were an example of COS's fourth priority: employee training and high morale. Pawley felt hourly workers would be a key ingredient in the long-term success of COS. At a Japanese company, like Toyota, workers might more easily accept a manufacturing system because "the manager is God, believe me. . . . But Americans, you have to sell them and you need to explain it," Pawley says. Even more important, the United Auto Workers was certain to consider many of COS's principles issues that would require union approval to implement. That would involve extensive negotiations and persuasion that Pawley did not want to attempt while COS was still being refined. Pawley instead concentrated on training his subordinates, or "direct reports" as they are called in Chrysler lingo, who then trained their subordinates, and on down to the assembly line, where individual groups of workers were picked to learn COS ideas before the system was implemented plantwide. (Union officials, curious about the concept, gave its limited use an okay while keeping the brakes on total acceptance. This allowed Pawley to get the bugs out without having to communicate COS to the entire plant.) The approach epitomized Chrysler's philosophy, called "waterfall communications." Even Eaton takes a turn teaching some courses, and being a student in others.

Inside Chrysler's manufacturing plants, COS is being taught on "lines of learning," each dedicated to a particular COS concept. It began with a single line in its St. Louis minivan plant. There, 30-year veteran autoworker Kenneth Chapman took charge of the assembly line's "quality alert system," Chrysler's variation on Toyota's *andon* cords. During a visit to the plant, I saw Chapman teaching his coworkers how to judge when to stop the line. It was a revelation to him: "I remember a time when they'd almost break your arm if you stopped the line. This makes you feel like more than just a number," Chapman says. By 1997, all of Chrysler's plants around the world had lines of learning. Its plant in Newark, Delaware, boasts four, as Pawley works to broaden the idea's acceptance.

By 1998, Pawley expects at least two brand new factories, in Kokomo, Indiana, and Campo Largo, Brazil, will make extensive use of COS principles. Further, Chrysler's new Toledo, Ohio, factory, set to open in 2000, is being designed to make maximum use of COS. "We are going to make these truly, truly world class operations," Pawley vows. Adds Eaton: "As you get more standardized, it becomes easier to do a plant in Argentina, or Brazil." In 1997, COS had already become so widely used within Chrysler that Pawley reassigned 20 of his 40-member COS teaching team to other tasks. Pawley says the effort is like a decathlon. "Nobody ever wins all 10 events. If you win three or four, and place high enough on the rest, you win the gold medal."

Driving him is the desire to equal Toyota's efficiency. Pawley says he realizes that it took Ohno 40 years to perfect TPS, but he thinks Chrysler is making quicker progress than Toyota did because it has Toyota's example to emulate. Says Pawley: "Sooner or later, I'm going to catch those suckers."

Toyota's Kitano isn't yielding the lead. But he believes Chrysler is on the right track by concentrating first on itself. "People would do better to focus on the [fundamentals]. If you try to do otherwise, you will fail. Your goal should be to be a strong manufacturer wherever you go. Globalization is secondary to that."

4

Global Innovation, at Home and Abroad

An early autumn haze hangs over the São Paulo skyline, a gray backdrop to the Brazilian city's tangled sprawl of skyscrapers and apartment buildings. As usual, traffic is clogged on the *marginal*, the main riverside road that is one of the few routes for drivers heading to the business district. Small Fiats and Volkswagens battle aggressively for road space with Chevrolets and Fords. Sitting in the back seat of his car as his driver maneuvers deftly through the crowded lanes, Dana Corporation's Latin American president, Cedomir Eterovic, smiles broadly.

"The more there are of them," he says, gesturing to the mess outside, "the more business it means for us."

Eterovic is taking a visitor to Osasco, a neighborhood on the outskirts of São Paulo that is home to one of

Dana's most significant and imaginative projects to date. Beginning in 1998, Dana's Osasco plant will produce what Dana calls a "rolling chassis" for the Dodge Dakota trucks that Chrysler will begin building at a new factory in Campo Largo, halfway between São Paulo and Brazil's southern border. Dana will provide virtually the entire underpinnings of those trucks, onto which Chrysler will add the engines and truck bodies. Almost 40 percent of the parts for the Dakota will come from Dana—the closest tie yet between Chrysler and a supplier, and the most content that Dana has yet provided to one of its customers in parts for a single product.

Dana's rolling chassis for Chrysler is just one example of the kind of opportunities that Vanguard companies are grasping with both hands. Vanguard members are using their global ventures as laboratories for new technology, new manufacturing processes, and new products. For them, going global is not just an opportunity to enter new markets, it is the chance to enhance their capabilities in the process.

Here are the stories of how global ventures have enhanced the competitiveness of Dana, Chrysler, Toyota, and Cummins, both at home and abroad.

Dana and the Rolling Chassis

Dana's Osasco plant sits behind an iron fence on lushly landscaped acreage dotted with wild hibiscus, impatiens, and hanging vines. Dana bought the property four years ago from Rockwell Automotive, which pulled out of Brazil in what turned out to be the final days of the nation's economic turmoil. Although it is the world's fifth largest country, with a population of over 150 million, skyrocketing inflation and interest rates, coupled with the impossibility of landing bank loans and credit, scared off innumerable investors in the early 1990s. In the darkest time, around 1992, inflation was averaging 2,000 percent a month. Residents of São Paulo joked that it was safest to pay for a taxi ride once you got in the car, since you might not be able to afford the fare when you reached your destination.

But in 1994, Brazilian President Fernando Collor got control over the country's financial crisis with a wide-ranging recovery program. He pegged Brazil's new currency, the *real*, to the U.S. dollar, and implemented a series of programs designed to encourage investment and economic stabilty. Inflation moderated, to about 8 percent in 1997, interest rates dropped from over 200 percent to a relatively modest 22 percent, per capital income climbed above $4,000 a household, nearly double that of China, and manufacturers were drawn back to Brazil in droves. Key players were the auto companies, who quickly had 15 new factories under construction. General Motors (GM), which had stuck with Brazil through its toughest days, announced expansion plans. So did Ford, which broke off a joint venture with Volkswagen to go it alone. So did Mercedes, Toyota, and Chrysler, which had dipped its toe in Latin American waters a few years earlier with a factory in Venezuela.

Buoyed by incentives to companies to build outside crowded São Paulo State, Brazil's traditional industrial heartland, Chrysler selected the Campo Largo site, gambling that Brazil would be a second hot market for its midsize Dakota, restyled for the United States in 1996. It was a somewhat risky bet, because small cars by far still dominate the Brazilian market. Yet, GM had seen success with its small Chevy Corsa pickup in Brazil, and Ford marketed its own small pickup, called

Courier, in 1997. Both appealed to increasingly well-heeled young Brazilians, who would load them up with sports gear and head to beaches for surfing or mountains for parasailing.

Still, there was a gap between those small trucks and the big sport utilities and pickups that both GM and Ford sold in limited numbers, mostly to commercial users. Chrysler saw this opening as market possibility and decided Campo Largo would be home to Dakota. But it wanted the venture to be as efficient as possible. It was aiming to keep pickup profit margins as high as the market would allow, and to quickly recover its $350 million Brazilian investment. Chrysler thought one answer might be "modular production," in which major portions of a vehicle are preassembled by suppliers and delivered to the plant. All Chrysler would then have to do was assemble these modules into a completed vehicle. The idea had been simmering for several years. In the late 1980s, Chrysler explored using modular methods to build a little Jeep, nicknamed the JJ, in a plant in Detroit. Dana was one of the suppliers involved in the project. But Chrysler was forced to cancel the program because it ultimately did not see enough demand for the little Jeeps. At that point, sport utilities were still used mostly for off-road adventure driving. They had not yet become the car substitutes that they turned into a few years later. Chrysler had also hit financial problems in the late 1980s. The company was being forced to focus its resources on volume sellers like sedans and minivans, and turn away from niche products like JJ.

But by late in the 1990s, Chrysler had shored up its balance sheet thanks to a strong lineup of popular vehicles like the Dodge Ram pickup, its minivans, and its Jeeps. These products were yielding the kind of cash that made it possible for Chrysler to pursue an overseas quest. As it looked at the Brazilian market, the company finally saw the opportunity to finally try out the modular idea that had been floating around its technical center for years. Says Dana CEO Southwood "Woody" Morcott: "When (automakers) go to some place like China or India or Brazil, they say to themselves, 'I don't need to do that here. I can get a supplier to do that.' "

Dana's Modular Systems Group, a collection of 204 people working in different sites around the world, came up with a design for Chrysler that combined the 178 parts used on the chassis of its U.S.-built Dakota into one unique module. Workers at Osasco will assemble an underbody that consists of the truck frame, rear axle, drive shaft, suspension, steering wheel, fuel tank, an underbody brace, fuel and electrical circuits, and wheels and tires. Together the parts comprise 38 percent of the total value of the truck, which costs about $17,000 in the United States and likely will sell in the $20,000 range in Brazil. And the chassis represents all the areas of Dana's expertise. "It's ultimate win for Dana," Morcott says.

Though the project would be unique in the world auto industry, Dana had built up its expertise with a similar rolling chassis that it supplied to Mack Truck in North America. However, there are significant differences. The Mack Truck chassis, used on heavy industrial trucks, is customized to order. Virtually every one of the 24,000 chassis made each year are different. The Dakota chassis, by contrast, will be mass produced at a potential volume three times what Dana builds for Mack.

For Chrysler, Dana's rolling chassis eliminates a number of headaches. Chrysler does not need to lay out space on the assembly plant floor that normally would be used to assemble the individual pieces of the chassis. It does not need to hire workers to assemble those parts, or to designate space in its stock room where the parts would be stored. It needs to designate only one receiving dock for trucks delivering the chassis. The modules can be rolled right to the assembly line at the point where they are needed. If there is a problem with any of the modules, Chrysler need only make a single phone call to Dana. And, unlike the United States, where such a project would cause political uproar among competing suppliers and the United Auto Workers union, there is nobody in Brazil to tell Chrysler and Dana that they can't do it.

"It's not an assembly issue. It's not displacing labor. It's a new model, a new platform, a new plant," says Dana Modular Systems Vice President Michael Laisure.

For Dana, the main advantage is obvious: it is providing a single module worth thousands of dollars to a major customer, capturing business it otherwise would have had to share. The project already is drawing industry experts to Osasco to see how the chassis is assembled. And Dana is benefiting: Laisure's group has 65 projects in various stages of development underway around the world.

Says Morcott: "The rolling chassis gets attention, draws people in to see it, improves our margins and satisfies a big customer."

Yet there are uncertainties. Any slowdown or shutdown at Osasco will quickly affect Chrysler's plant. Dana must keep close watch on the quality and delivery of the parts it receives from its own suppliers for the rolling chassis. And Dana's own investment rides on Dakota's success. "It's a bit of a risk for us," Morcott says. "If their vehicle doesn't sell, if they have an Edsel in Brazil, you've made an investment that you can't recoup."

Chrysler, for its part, isn't concerned whether Dana can pull its weight. "You don't have a relationship where [a component] shows up at the door and you say, 'what the heck is this?' " says Advanced Manufacturing Director Frank Ewasyshyn. "You're talking all the way from the beginning. You're sharing problems, you're sharing issues. When you do that, the disasters don't happen."

CHRYSLER IN GRAZ

But Chrysler would not even be considering building a new plant in Brazil, or using an innovative chassis designed by Dana, if it had not been for the success of its groundbreaking manufacturing venture in Graz, Austria. In a joint arrangement with veteran European body builder Steyr-Daimler-Puch, Chrysler builds Jeep Grand Cherokees and Voyager minivans that are virtually identical to the vehicles produced at its plants in North America, save for modifications required in various European markets to parts such as headlights and mirrors. The Voyager project has particular significance because Graz (pronounced Gratz) is part of a three-member family of Chrysler plants, all producing minivans.

The blue and white Eurostar plant, nestled in Alpine foothills about three hours from Vienna, is a miniature version of Chrysler's mammoth minivan plants in St. Louis, Missouri, and Windsor, Ontario. The Voyagers coming off the assembly line appear exactly the same, down to the cup holders. Workers in coveralls and lab coats perform the same tasks and receive the same training as their colleagues across the Atlantic. Only the jar of *Alpenmilch* on the coffee cart in plant manager Don Manvel's office, and the *Creditanstalt* bank branch in the lobby (giving away watches to new account holders) provide a hint that the factory is half a world away from its counterparts.

"We are the third sister, albeit the little sister," Manvel says.[1] "Little" seems to be the operative word: With about 1,500 workers, Eurostar can produce 50,000 minivans a year, only 20 percent of the capacity of one of Chrysler's North American plants, which hum day and night on three shifts. Yet Eurostar is the linchpin of Chrysler's carefully edited strategy of putting a limited number of plants in key global locations. "Graz has been an outstanding success for us," says Chrysler CEO Robert Eaton. "It has allowed us to do things that would be much more expensive if we tried to do them at home."

In the case of the minivans, that includes right-hand drive vehicles for England, Japan, and Australia, as well as diesel-equipped vans for which there is little demand in the United States, but significant appeal in other parts of the world. "The high volume plants, you want them to build the bread and butter minivans, the low complexity vehicles, and just shoot them down the line. We've taken over the complexity here with our lower volume. We have the diesel engine, we have the right-hand-drive," explains Manvel.

Chrysler broke ground for the Graz venture in 1990, two years before Eaton left GM's European operations to succeed Lee Iacocca as CEO. At that time, Chrysler was in the early stages of a bid to expand its European sales, primarily through exports from North America. The minivan market, already over 1 million vehicles in the United States, was in its fledgling stages in Europe. Only Renault, with a boxy van called Espace, had made a sales dent. Vehicles from Ford, Volkswagen, and Opel were still years away. Iacocca, who had long wanted to make an impact in the then-burgeoning European car market, saw an opportunity for Chrysler in the developing minivan niche. Buoyed by the Graz-built minivans, Chrysler's European sales, including imports of North American-built autos, climbed from 41,000 vehicles in 1990 to 67,000 in 1994 and broke 102,000 in 1996.

Initially, Graz was conceived as merely a step up from a "screwdriver plant," where vehicles are assembled from kits of parts shipped from another factory. These CKD (complete knockdown) factories are often an easy way into markets where a manufacturer is hesitant to build a full-fledged facility because of uncertainty about the supply lines or its partner. True, Chrysler had little to fear from linking up with Steyr. Steyr does engineering work for 15 major manufacturers, and builds sport utilities for partner Mercedes-Benz at the same Graz plant where it added Jeep production in 1994. Chrysler showed its confidence in Graz's potential by constructing small body and paint shops, and a complete final assembly line. But, unsure of local suppliers' quality, Chrysler still shipped in many of the parts for its minivans and Jeeps.

As Chrysler prepared to introduce a new family of minivans in late 1995, executive vice president Dennis Pawley and minivan platform director Christopher Theodore felt Graz could play a greater role. They decided it was ready to build minivans according to the same processes Chrysler used in North America, including some features of the new Chrysler Operating System. Meanwhile, Chrysler's own suppliers and those of competing European auto companies had begun opening plants in the area, drawn by the Graz plant. Chrysler felt more confident that local parts could meet its standards and decided it would cut back on its parts imports.

"We are the top employer in town. We've very greatly changed the employment structure of the area, because we've brought a number of suppliers with us," Manvel explains.

Given Graz's development beyond the screwdriver stage, Chrysler decided the minivans' launch would be carried out according to a carefully timed cadence. St. Louis became the "lead" plant on the project. It served as a manufacturing laboratory for production of the new minivans and got to build them first, in late spring of 1995. Teams from Graz and Windsor worked on the assembly line alongside their St. Louis counterparts, learning the changes that the production would bring first. Then, using lessons learned in St. Louis, Windsor added the vans in fall 1995. And just a few months later, Graz began building them, using virtually the same processes, material flow to the assembly line, and worker training as its sister plants.

By that point, Chrysler had already incorporated the Graz plant into its information network. The first sound a visitor notices sitting in Manvel's office is a frequent "beep" from his computer screen. The sound signals an update from Chrysler of sales figures or production numbers. Walking over to demonstrate, Manvel uses his computer mouse to pull up a screen that shows current production numbers for the St. Louis plant. Then he clicks on a heading that brings up numbers for Windsor's production at that moment. The information comes from Chrysler's main data center in Belvidere, Illinois, which links all the company's plants around the world. If he wishes, Manvel can also see how pickup truck production is proceeding in Sterling Heights, Michigan, or monitor the pace of cars rolling off the assembly line in Bramalea, Ontario.

"To me, it's just amazing that we run this plant from

a data system in Belvidere, Illinois. We are never, ever down. It is not like we are shutting this plant down because we can't get into the computer," Manvel says.

The system is far more than a source for statistics: Plant managers and engineers constantly e-mail one another with suggestions for improvements and solutions to problems. That day, a Chrysler engineer was at work in the Graz plant, putting in a new fixture for installing the minivans' sliding doors. The fixture had been developed the week before in Windsor, and engineers were dispatched to St. Louis and Graz to make similar changes on those plants' assembly lines. Often, instead of a physical visit, Chrysler engineers and manufacturing experts gather via video conferencing to share experiences and diagnose problems. "It really speeds communications," Manvel says.

Graz has contributed its own share of changes. Inside the factory, Graz has set up lines of learning that are its own on-site laboratories for new ideas. It discovered that workers who assemble doors at Graz were frustrated because they could not find the parts they needed when they needed them. Each had to spend time rummaging for the correct screws and supplies among more than 100 bins of parts stacked behind the assembly line.

To solve the problem, workers moved the bins to either end of the assembly line. Then, they went to a local hardware store and bought plastic crates, like those children use to store their toys. They filled one stack with the parts needed to assemble doors during one eight-hour shift. Now, at the start of each shift, a team member goes "shopping" to stack rolling cars with parts that will be needed during the day. Each car carries a Polaroid photo showing the necessary parts and how they should be arranged. The carriers are then stationed in areas marked off with color-coded tape. It is the same kind of a solution that a materials specialist could have prescribed, but the answer at Graz was deduced by a team of former waitresses and farmers.

"I like not having parts near the assembly line. They got in my way," says door line worker Regina Krause. During a pause from wielding a hydraulic drill, Krause laughs when she is asked why she came to work for Chrysler. "To have more money for shopping," she says, and to pay for an apartment she recently purchased with her husband, also a worker in the plant.

Manvel sings the praises of the workforce, which is arranged in work teams of 8 to 15 people each. Chrysler discovered teams feel tremendous loyalty to their team leaders, and prefer to get information about company policies and training methods directly from them rather than through company memos. This process fits nicely with Chrysler's philosophy of "waterfall communications," in which concepts spill down from management to workers in a continuous flow. "Any problems that might occur, the operator will call the team leader over to get it resolved. If they need to, they go to an engineer, with the production concept being 'Get it right, within the zone, before it moves on,' " Manvel says.

However, the decision-making authority also can go to extremes. Neatniks on one maintenance crew kept wiping production equipment clean, frustrating engineers who used oil leaks as indications of potential problems. "We had to tell them, 'Don't clean the machine so much—if there's a leak, we need to see it,' " Manvel says, smiling.

This can-do attitude extends to management as well. As it was preparing to expand its paint shop in Graz for the next-generation minivans, Chrysler officials discovered the change required national environmental permits that might take up to three years to acquire. Instead of halting the construction, which would have disrupted the minivans' launch, plant officials, working with local authorities, invited eight bureaucrats responsible for the permits to visit the Graz plant. It set up a conference room with desks for each official, arranged in the order in which permits had to be obtained. When a question arose about a Chrysler procedure, a plant official took the bureaucrat to the factory floor, or called an engineer to explain what the company was doing.

"We got our operating permits in three days. And we had a little celebration," Manvel recalls. The red-tape slicing proved so popular that Austrian officials now use the experience as a selling tool to lure potential manufacturing investments.

Chrysler eventually hopes to apply for more permits in Graz so that it can add a third shift of workers and increase production to 80,000 a year. It is not yet there. The European auto market turned sluggish in 1996, leaving Chrysler's minivan sales stalled at about 40,000 a year. As a result, the plant has not yet reached its full production of 50,000 a year. Yet, Chrysler has shown faith in Graz's potential by announcing it will soon purchase all its stamped components—metal panels, doors, hoods, roofs, and other parts—from local vendors. Regardless of its sales levels, Graz has proved to be a valuable global learning tool for Chrysler—and for its competition.

TOYOTA SIENNA IN GEORGETOWN

In late 1997, Toyota drew from Chrysler's minivan expertise to pull off one of the biggest global manufacturing gambles in its history. At its sprawling George-town, Kentucky, complex, Toyota began building the Sienna minivan alongside the Camry sedan. In doing so, Toyota became only the world's second automaker to build minivans and cars on the same assembly line. Only Mazda, at its Ujina plant near Hiroshima, Japan, had ever tried it before, building its MPV on a line with five other vehicles.

"This is the biggest manufacturing challenge of my career," says Georgetown Manufacturing Vice President Michael DaPrile, a 10-year Toyota veteran who spent more than two decades at GM.

DaPrile, one of the highest-ranking Americans in the Toyota system, has helped turn Georgetown into a manufacturing showcase. Where experts and industry rivals flocked to Japanese Toyota plants in Motomachi, Tahara, and Toyota City in the 1970s and 1980s, by the late 1990s they were descending instead upon George-town. Begun in 1986 with a single assembly plant employing 2,000 workers, Georgetown had grown by 1997 to 7,500 workers at two assembly plants, an engine plant, a test track, and a plastics operation making everything from bumpers to instrument panels. Every single person working in the complex, from factory worker to executive, had been trained in the Toyota Production System. Toyota's Supplier Support Center bustled day and evening teaching the system to Toyota's parts suppliers as well as to other companies that wanted to explore what had made Toyota so success-ful.

Yet for all its manufacturing expertise, Japan's premiere auto company had never been more than an also-ran in minivans. From 1982 through 1997, Toyota relied on the Previa, designed to be a niche vehicle in Japan where minivans were more of a curiosity than the volume sellers they had become in the United States. Odd-looking Previa, which cost upward of $25,000 by the late 1990s, was priced well above its competition and lacked features such as cup holders and compasses that American consumers had come to demand. Toyota did not even build Previa itself: the van was built by sub-contractor Hino Motors and by Toyota's auto body making unit. So the knowledge to build a minivan did not reside within the company. And without it, Toyota officials knew they could never hope to build a com-petitive product that could make a respectable show-ing in the U.S. minivan market and in Europe, where minivan sales had exploded to over 1 million vehicles a year, most of them Chrysler's products.

So Toyota turned to Chrysler for help—a surprising move, given the pace of competition in the auto indus-try, but in fact Chrysler's assistance was quid pro quo for the help Toyota had given Chrysler in creating COS. From 1995 to 1997, Chrysler let Toyota managers and workers tour Chrysler minivan plants, looking for ways to ease Sienna production. From Chrysler came ideas on how to install three rows of seats, full-length trim panels and large pieces of carpet. "Chrysler gave us a lot of help," Mike DaPrile acknowledges. Replies Chrysler Executive Vice President Dennis Pawley, "We have far more to learn from them than they do from us." Such cooperation could not have occurred at the start of the 1990s, says University of Michigan automo-tive expert David Cole. "A few years ago, there was a wall between the companies. This would have been im-possible," Cole says.

But both Toyota and Chrysler have something to gain by working together, Cole says: "It's not a one-way communication flow. You share and you learn. And if you become a little smarter, it's worth it." In addition, he adds, "Generally, the more confident you are about your expertise, the less secrecy you have about it."

Chrysler Minivan Vice President Shamuel Rushwin notes many automakers still wouldn't want to admit they asked for help from a competitor. "We have this built-in resistance to copying somebody else. I'd prefer to call it 'creative swiping.' Why should we have to come up with solutions on our own?" Rushwin says. Starting with only knowledge of how to build sedans, the visits to St. Louis, Windsor, and Graz yielded DaPrile, Georgetown Plant Manager Cheryl Jones, and Toyota engineers and workers hundreds of hints on assembling a minivan. But ultimately Chrysler, whose minivan plants build only minivans, couldn't help Toyota solve its fundamental problem of producing a car and a small van on the same assembly line. Even though the two vehicles were based on the same chassis, size alone dictated a number of different parts. Only about 40 percent of the vehicles' components would be shared.

"My first reaction when I heard that they were going to try it was, 'Wow,' " says Pawley.

Increasingly there was pressure from Toyota's desire for production to begin quickly. Camry, the best-selling car in the United States in 1997, was flying out of showrooms. And even though Toyota was also building them at its second Georgetown assembly plant with full-size Avalon sedans, any delays foisted by the addition of Sienna would cut into Camry sales. "The way Camry is selling now, we wanted to what was best for Camry and best for the minivan," Jones says.

She and DaPrile tried to make the transformation as smooth as possible. The first step: Highlight the spots on the assembly line where the most significant differences between the vehicles would take place. Out of

300 stations on the assembly line, Toyota found Sienna required different parts at 26. But only seven all-new production steps were needed, including the installation of sliding doors, carpet, roof lining, rear seats, and roof racks. In a bid to save on production time, Toyota chose not to add new work stations. Instead, it selected two teams of workers, one for each shift, who would be responsible for attaching Sienna-only parts. Meanwhile, engineers working with Toyota workers on the factory floor designed equipment intended to make those duties easy to perform.

As soon as a Sienna approaches one of the seven spots on the assembly line, a member of the Sienna team is there to take over. Some team members climb inside, where they scoot around on wheeled carts that look like NASA's Sojourner Mars explorer. These workers handle installation of the minivan's ceiling, a seven-foot-long piece of insulation and fabric called a headliner. Others help adjust and attach the instrument panel, which runs the full width of the van. Outside, workers stand on special platforms to attach the minivans' roof racks. The platforms put the roof waist high, eliminating the need to reach. Toyota also developed special dollies that swing the van's heavy, sliding doors directly to connecting brackets on either side of the van, so workers do not have to lift the doors. Once connected, the doors must slide smoothly down tracks on either side of the car. Even days before production began, Toyota was still refining the process, which it had laid out in a special work area near the assembly line where machinery had been installed. "That was one of the hardest to figure out," Jones admits.

But, says the University of Michigan's Cole, "It's a whole lot easier if you have the set of common processes and systems that Toyota has." Ultimately, it took just 45 days for production of Siennas to hit full line-speed, enhancing Georgetown's reputation as a premier global manufacturing complex. DaPrile, who had suffered through generations of botched new-product launches at GM, where plants still require a year or more to reach forecast production levels, shakes his head. "There's something special going on here," he says.

THE CUMMINS MID-RANGE ENGINE PLANT

In 1991, Cummins Engine faced a decision: Heavy demand for its global diesel engine, the B-series, meant it would need to increase production. Used on pickup trucks, the engine, which ranged from 56 to 230 horsepower, was already being made at Cummins plants in England and Brazil. A joint venture in India was under development and the B-series seemed a perfect product for a market that company executives felt was about to explode. As Cummins's engine division managers debated the location of a B-series production site, the only place that seemed unlikely for the new B-engine plant was Cummins's home market, the United States, where Cummins felt it had plenty of capacity. "We could have put it anywhere. We didn't need to put it here," says Cummins Executive Vice President Joseph Loughrey.

Ultimately, however, Cummins chose to reopen an assembly plant in its Indiana backyard. The decision led to a transformation of the methods Cummins uses to develop and assemble its products, and it significantly changed the role that its workers play in its manufacturing operations. Those changes, which took root at Cummins's Mid-Range Engine Plant in Columbus, Indiana, have since spread to Cummins's 40 plants around the world, helping to increase Cummins's productivity and efficiency.

As Cummins was trying to decide where to expand B-series engine production, Loughrey and a group of company managers had completed more than two years of work drafting the Cummins Production System. In early 1991, the company's plant managers had begun implementing aspects of the system in pilot projects. Despite some initial skepticism, Loughrey was pleased with how quickly the concept was spreading, first to three plants and then to 10 by the year's end. But he longed for one plant that would act as a laboratory for CPS and for a team-based work system. During his many trips to establish benchmarks for CPS, Loughrey had been impressed by the improvements in efficiency and quality that he had encountered at NUMMI, the joint venture between GM and Toyota in Fremont, California, and at Toyota's Georgetown, Kentucky, plant. At both, groups of workers were responsible for finding quick solutions to problems that occurred on the assembly line and encouraged to make suggestions on how their jobs could be improved. Each team member also was expected to keep learning new skills and to teach those skills to less experienced team members. Soon, the most famous application of this team process, GM's small car factory, Saturn, in Spring Hill, Tennessee, would come to the forefront. But Saturn was still in its infancy when Loughrey was mulling his idea for his own testing ground.

Loughrey knew it would be much easier to implement the CPS concepts at a brand new plant, with a new workforce whose members had been selected because of their openness to trying a team approach. (This is what would later be done with great success at GM's Saturn factory.) But Cummins, which had skirted several financial crises in the 1980s, had no intention of building a "greenfield" plant in North America just so that Loughrey could test out his theories. Loughrey would have to make do with one of Cummins's existing "brownfield" factories, even though the pilot CPS projects had demonstrated how difficult it would be to simply throw out a plant's entire work system and replace it with all new methods overnight.

Cummins chose two plants as possible testing grounds, one in Alabama and the other, CMEP, just 10 minutes from Cummins's headquarters. Alabama workers turned the company's offer down, and attention turned to CMEP, which had closed in 1988, only 16 years after it had been built. Set on the outskirts of Columbus, the building was one of the company's and the town's architectural jewels. It was a dramatic departure from the low-rise, wide-slung boxes that define manufacturing in the late 20th century. The 450,000 square foot factory was designed in 1972 by architect Kevin Roche, better known for office buildings that emphasize the use of natural light. The glass-sided building's unique layout gives a view of the outside world from anywhere in the plant. It uses a minimum of interior supports, so that it is easy to see straight down the assembly line, and across the plant from side to side. Even the entrance is unique. Because the plant is built into a berm, visitors drive up ramps to park on the roof, then take elevators to the plant floor. While in most plants offices are perched high above the assembly line, so that managers can gaze down at the activity below, CMEP's few offices are on an eye-level mezzanine, up just a handful of steps from the factory floor.

Unfortunately for Cummins, the quality of the building's design had never been matched by the quality of the engines built there. More than 3,000 workers had crowded into the plant, building 400 engines a day. But defects were well above what Cummins's customers deemed acceptable, causing Cummins to slash production and jobs. By the late 1980s, faced with a financial crunch, stiff competition from Japanese rivals, and too much engine capacity, Cummins decided to close the factory and lay off the remaining 1,200 workers. "If we weren't there, we were drifting towards uncompetitiveness," Loughrey says. The shutdown was a heavy blow to a town of 30,000 people where Cummins was by far the largest employer. Officials of the Diesel-workers Union (DWU), concerned by Cummins's growing investments outside the United States, had repeatedly demanded during contract negotiations that the plant be reopened. But even in the most recent round of talks, in 1990, Cummins had refused.

Now, with Alabama workers rejecting the chance to be a CPS testing ground, Cummins decided CMEP would become a "greenfield brownfield plant" where CPS could be implemented all at once. "We had the umbrella and the time frame to make it work," Loughrey says. Quietly, he began overtures to then-DWU President Larry Neihart. During the 1990 negotiations, the pair had begun meeting every Wednesday morning at 6 o'clock for an hour, just to talk about issues on their minds. "The idea was that this was not a grievance session. We didn't bring grievances to the floor. Once in a while, he might point out, 'there's this problem, it's coming your way.' . . . but we didn't use the time for that. It was more to talk about the business, who the competition was, where are things really going in the future. It led to a series of understandings about what it was going to take to be successful," Loughrey says.

It was at one of these breakfasts, in early 1991, that Loughrey gingerly brought up the topic of CMEP. He felt strongly that Cummins could not merely recall the 1,200 laid-off workers, who would expect that their jobs would be the same as they always were. Loughrey insisted that the workers go through an assessment program that would teach them the principles of CPS, and determine who would be most comfortable in a team-based work system. Further, Cummins could only promise that 500 of the workers would land jobs immediately. Long-term, it hoped that new business would lead to an increase in line speed at the plant, prompting more rehiring. But early on, it could only offer one shift a chance to return.

Union leaders agreed to the testing program, thinking it was going to be a formality. In retrospect, "We didn't realize how rough it was going to be to get through the assessment program. We probably didn't look close enough in negotiations," says Neihart.

Cummins's other condition was a separate contract covering only the CMEP workers that would spell out what was expected of them under CPS. Other Cummins plants had a half a dozen job classifications, which were a common union tactic that limited the tasks that workers could perform so that a company was forced to hire more people. At CMEP, Cummins planned to have just two job classifications—assembler and specialist, the equivalent of a skilled-trades worker at a typical Cummins plant. Specialists would earn 25 cents an hour more than assemblers, while workers chosen by their peers to be team leaders would earn 50 cents more.

Neihart saw trouble. He feared an uproar, not only from the 1,200 idled workers but from the rest of the Cummins workforce. He knew veteran workers at other plants would fear that their own pay and even their jobs would be in jeopardy, once Cummins began implementing the new work system. Yet, by that point, economic conditions at Cummins and in the United States were uncertain. U.S. auto sales had slipped, and tension was building in the Middle East, where Iraq was only months away from invading Kuwait. Neihart knew that if he rejected Cummins's proposal, CMEP might never reopen, and production of the B-engine and other company products might go halfway around the globe.

On the advice of the DWU's attorney, Neihart suggested asking Cummins's entire southern Indiana workforce of 14,000 people to vote on the contract proposal for CMEP, so that even workers who would not set foot in the plant would feel comfortable with the situation their colleagues faced. (Ironically, workers laid off from the plant were not eligible to vote on the proposal since they were not members in good standing of the DWU.) Cummins agreed. Though the proposal sparked heated debate, the vote was almost an anticlimax: The proposal passed by a margin of four to one.

Says the union leader, "I made a lot of bad decisions in my time but that wasn't one of them. I still think it was the right thing to do, no matter how much criticism I took." Less than a year later, in 1992, Cummins reopened the plant, implementing its CPS principles overnight. The 10 practices were posted on the walls around the plant and handed to every worker on tri-folded pocket cards. The rehired workers had already undergone 128 hours of training in CPS and the team-based concept.

The first test of Cummins's commitment to the system came quickly. During training, each worker had to build 15 test engines apiece over a two-day period. Right away, workers raised objections to the way engineers had laid out the factory floor. They asked for changes that would require a near-complete redesign of what had taken months for the manufacturing experts to install.

"We said, 'okay.' " says Loughrey. That earned Cummins officials' credibility in the workers' eyes. "They said, 'Maybe they are serious about having us work harder. Maybe, this might be something we are willing to take a risk on in southern Indiana,' " he adds.

Using workers' suggestions, and the key CPS concept of continuous flow, engineers eliminated the assembly line's twists and turns. As a result, once an engine starts its journey at the west end of the plant, it never retraces its steps. It winds forward through work stations spaced 15 feet apart, makes a left turn and proceeds into the paint shop, passes through a testing area, then exits at the north end of the plant where it is loaded onto a delivery truck, in the sequence in which it will be needed when it arrives at a customer's plant. The pace at which the plant is progressing is reflected on *andon* boards posted above sections of the assembly line that show the day's production goal and how many engines have been built at that point.

Except for rolling carts stocked with the parts workers will need that shift, there is no inventory in sight. The plant has no buffer zone; less than two hours of parts are on hand throughout the facility. This causes some managers to lose sleep, for when there is a glitch anywhere in the system, either at one of the 300 suppliers providing parts to Cummins, or at one of its customers, the impact at CMEP is dramatic. For example, production fell dramatically during May 1997, when Chrysler, Cummins's biggest B-series customer, was hit by a month-long United Auto Workers strike that shut its truck plants. It took the plant until July to return to full capacity.

But by that time, CMEP was bringing on a second

shift of 500 workers. Cummins had landed new diesel engine business with Ford for its F-series truck, thanks in part to Chrysler's satisfaction with the B-series engines Cummins made for its Ram pickups. The second shift would bring the plant to 1,000 workers making 1,000 engines a day. All of the new employees were undergoing the same CPS training that the plant's original workforce had undergone, but with a difference: Some of the classes and workshops were being taught by the Cummins workers themselves, now well schooled in the principles of CPS.

The newcomers were made to feel at home: Photos of all the workers in the plant are displayed on a big bulletin board at the front of the building, and every work team has its own board listing the names and duties of every team member. Though the plant has a canteen, workers are encouraged to lunch together at tables and chairs set behind dividers near the assembly line. Plant managers, dressed in the same khaki pants and buttoned-down white shirts as team members, frequently walk the plant's spotless floors, greeting workers by name and engaging them in conversation.

"We chose to believe that an older workforce could understand, begin to adapt to and eventually lead an effort to change the work system to make things better. And that's happened," Loughrey says.

5

The Surprise Battleground

In late summer 1993, Mercedes-Benz officials sat in a conference room in the company's headquarters at Unterterkheim, Germany, outside Stuttgart, facing a key decision. The luxury automaker, renowned around the world for its solid, high-quality, high-performance sedans and sports cars, had nonetheless been hammered in the early 1990s by industry downturns in Europe and the United States, its two key markets. Its latest generation of cars, the top-end S-class sedans, had just been introduced in a shower of criticism—both for their $100,000-plus price tag and the 100-plus hours that each took to build. At a time when nimble Japanese companies like Toyota and Honda were setting new productivity standards, turning out even their luxury cars in 35 hours or less, Mercedes was in danger of becoming a German anachronism.

A new generation of company executives at Mercedes, alarmed by the picture before them, decided it was time to change. "We had become a little bit lazy—I'm glad to say it," says Juergen Hubbert, then in charge of product development and now automotive chief for parent Daimler-Benz. "It was difficult to do. People were saying to us, 'stop, stop, stop, the good days will come back.' We said, 'No, they will never come back.' "

Among the changes that Hubbert was proposing was a trio of new vehicles, each to be built in all new or overhauled factories, each a sharp departure from Mercedes's upper-level luxury car heritage. Mercedes had already startled its competition by disclosing that it was teaming with spunky Swiss watchmaker Swatch to bring out the Smart car, a fun minimobile aimed at Generation X city dwellers. A second small car, called the A-class, would be aimed at entry-level buyers whom Mercedes needed to attract in order to expand its sales, but who did not want to spend the minimum $30,000 that a Mercedes car then cost.

The third project lay before the executives this day in Unterterkheim: a car-like, luxury sport utility vehicle, aimed squarely at the exploding SUV market that had developed in the United States and that was showing signs of expanding elsewhere. Mercedes research showed that a staggering 30 percent of its U.S. owners also had sport utilities parked in their driveways, built by competitors such as Range Rover, Jeep, and Ford. Mercedes sold roughly 100,000 vehicles a year in the United States, so the defections represented 30,000 chances a year at selling another Mercedes. And there were signs Mercedes stood to lose further opportunities in Europe, because Chrysler was about to begin building Jeeps in Graz, Austria.

In January 1993, Mercedes's board had given the go-ahead to a luxury sport utility, called M-class. That spring, the company disclosed it would be built in North America, not Germany. At home, Mercedes's labor rates had soared well above $47 an hour, the highest in the world for an automaker. The labor contracts at its plants in German stymied efforts to introduce efficient manufacturing concepts.

Workers in Germany spent only about 34 hours a week on the job, or about 1,700 hours a year, compared with 40 hours a week, or 2,000 a year, in the United States. In a typical eight-hour shift, consisting of 480 minutes on the job, Mercedes could count on getting only about 340 minutes or 5.6 hours of work because of strict union regulations that required at least 90 minutes for lunch, plus two additional breaks. In the United States, that same 480 minutes on the job yielded about 440 minutes or 7.3 hours of work time, due to shorter lunch and break times. Further, Saturday overtime in Germany was banned by Mercedes's works council. Workers' schedules could not be changed without permission. And the strict work rules limited the number of tasks each workers was required to learn. Company surveys showed Mercedes plants in Germany were 30 percent less productive overall than the best Japanese and U.S. plants.

As word leaked that Mercedes was considering North American plant sites, it was deluged with offers. If Mercedes wanted to really save money, it could go to Mexico, where labor rates were a mere $2 an hour. But that option was quickly discarded. Says author James Womack: "If you're Mercedes and you're worried about upholding your image, the Mexico thing doesn't sound quite right." Besides, more than 150 U.S. sites alone vied for the plant, from Nebraska to the Carolinas. Following the lead of chief competitor BMW, which in 1992 had selected Greer, South Carolina as the site of its first U.S. factory, Mercedes headed to the American South. In September 1993, the company announced its $350 million, 1 million square-foot plant would be built in Vance, Alabama, outside Tuscaloosa, hundreds of miles away from automotive centers like Detroit, St. Louis, and Cleveland.

Says Hubbert: "We wanted a new product, new people, a new country, doing things in an entirely new way."

Today, Mercedes's $1.1 billion decision stands as an illustration of the ability of the United States to compete in the global manufacturing arena. While for years U.S. companies have been hurtling across their own country's borders to invest elsewhere, the world's most successful manufacturers see the necessity of investing in the United States. More than $86 billion in direct manufacturing investment was made in 1996 alone by companies based in countries from Korea to Germany, Italy to Brazil. The United States has become Honda's single most important world market, exceeding even Japan. Honda is able to design, engineer, and manufacture vehicles at its operations in Michigan, California, and Ohio. In 1997, it broke new ground with the latest version of its midsize Accord, built at its plant in Marysville, Ohio. Accord became the first car completely developed and manufactured in the United States for U.S. consumers. Nearly 98 percent of its parts are sourced in the United States. Even Toyota still performs much of its engineering and development work in Japan, and its Camry, built in Georgetown, Kentucky, is only about 66 percent U.S. content.

Regardless, both Ohio-built Accords and Kentucky-built Camrys have been seamlessly substituted in buyers' minds for the Japanese-built cars they replaced in their companies' respective lineups. "People don't argue about that any more. There is no question you can do anything you can do at Toyota in Japan at Georgetown," says author James Womack.

But there is a fundamental difference between why Honda and Toyota set up their U.S. operations and the reason BMW and Mercedes are here. In the 1980s, when the bulk of their products were made overseas, Japanese companies faced severe political pressure to build plants here or face stiff import quotas. In the 1990s, nobody is threatening German luxury car makers with sanctions. Nobody is forcing any non-U.S. manufacturers to set up shop anyplace in the United States. They are here because they see clear market advantages to being here and because these plants fit into their global expansion strategies.

"If you succeed in the U.S., you have succeeded in an unprotected, cutthroat, extremely competitive market, and your whole group gains," says Percy Barnevik, CEO of Sweden's Investor.[1]

Adds Renault Executive Vice President Carlos Ghosn, "You cannot call yourself a global company if you do not manufacture in North America." Despite its operations in Europe, Latin America, and China, Renault does not feel it has the right product or capabilities to operate a plant in the United States. And thus, Ghosn says, Renault is not a global manufacturer.

"The United States is as good a place as any to have manufacturing operations. You have a country with a strong economy. You can get incentives from any state. And you are going in as king of the local market and you can cherry-pick the best workers," says David

Cole, director of the Office for the Study of Automotive Transportation at the University of Michigan.

Though many U.S. manufacturers still grumble about high labor costs, the world's manufacturers have a different basis of comparison. A 1997 study by ITT Industries, maker of a wide range of auto parts and components, showed that company's highest costs were actually at a plant in Gifhorn, Germany, where workers earned an average $41.50 an hour in wages and fringe benefits. ITT's largest U.S. operation, in Rochester, New York, paid its workers nearly $10 an hour less, even though they are members of the United Auto Workers and enjoy benefits such as fully paid health care. But at a nonunion plant in Asheville, North Carolina, ITT pays its workers just under $14 an hour, less than the company pays workers in Brazil and Spain, two countries known to be relatively cheap places to do business. Even by averaging its most expensive facility, Rochester, with its cheapest U.S. plant, Asheville, ITT still can manufacture components in the U.S. for under $20 an hour, competitive by the standards of any semi-developed country.

The key, says Lehman Brothers Senior Vice President Joseph Phillippi, is attitude—on the part of the company and of its workers. "The Germans and the Japanese and even our companies have all proven that if you go in with a clean sheet of paper, a workforce that has no preconceived notions of what is right or wrong on the factory floor, these plants can be as efficient and productive as any of their plants elsewhere in the world."

When it came time for Cummins Engine to find a spot for its fuel-efficient Signature 600 engine, aimed at tractor trailer operators, the choice of a production site was simple: Columbus, Indiana. "A majority of its production will be aimed at customers in North America, so it makes sense to invest in North America," explains Cummins Chief Financial Officer Kirin Patel. "What's the market, and what's the best place to support the market? We aren't trying to strike any ratios" between U.S. and non-U.S. manufacturing operations, Patel adds.

Admittedly, one of the biggest draws for non-U.S. manufacturers has been the attractive incentive packages that states have offered to win the companys' investments. Alabama, home to the new Mercedes plant, stands out as what some experts would say is an example of excess. To land the plant, it offered tax incentives, road improvements, training programs, and other perks valued at about $350 million, roughly $200,000 per job or 25 percent of what Mercedes itself was investing in the entire project. The subsidies were more than double the $150 million that South Carolina offered in 1992 for the BWM plant, and almost triple the $125 million Kentucky paid to secure Toyota's original Georgetown investment. And the Alabama deal dwarfs the mere $5 million in tax breaks that Honda originally got from the state of Ohio to build its first factory in Marysville in 1982.

But these states all consider the money well spent, because these investments have invariably led to more of the same. South Carolina in particular can boast a manufacturing investment climate unrivaled by other states, and even some small countries. In 1996 alone, it secured $5.7 billion in new manufacturing investment, generating 26,000 new manufacturing jobs. Of that total, $2.2 billion came from non-U.S. companies employing 5,000 workers. Both the dollar investment and the job creation put South Carolina atop the 50 states in new manufacturing ventures. And from 1960 to 1996, South Carolina had attracted a total of $14 billion in non-U.S. investment, leading to the creation of 78,195 jobs at non-U.S. owned companies.

The biggest non-U.S. investor in South Carolina in 1996 was not BMW, even though the German carmaker's decision to build flashy Z3 sportscars in Greer had thrown a spotlight on the state as a hotbed of international investment. Its top investor was German chemical and fabric company Hoechst Celanese Corporation, which poured $350 million into expanded an existing polyester factory in Spartanburg. The state's list of investors in 1996 alone runs the gamut from Hoescht and BWM to Japan's Fuji Film, Canada's Samuel Strapping Systems, makers of plastic container straps, Switzerland's Schweizerhall chemical company, and Italy's Gividi USA, which makes woven fiberglass fabric.

Though 85 percent of the year's investment came from companies already settled in South Carolina, 22 new international companies came in 1996, bringing $250 million in investments and 1,446 new jobs. The reasons ranged from state incentive packages to the state's lack of unions to its three seaports to the need to be near big customers, such as the auto suppliers who came to the state upon the heels of BMW. The state lures them with trade missions, often arranged by its office in Frankfurt, Germany; a computerized database of investment opportunities; and a team of investment specialists devoted to finding potential investors. In 1990, South Carolina's export office got only 25 calls a week; in 1997, it was fielding four times as many.

The flood of investments to a state whose major industries 30 years ago were farming and textiles has helped make up for losing the Mercedes factory to Alabama, which had already attracted electronics firms to Huntsville and steel makers to Birmingham.

The Mercedes factory in tiny Vance, population 400, is not all that easy to reach—perhaps by design. Getting there requires changing planes in Atlanta for a quick hop to Birmingham. Then it's an hour's drive southwest on I-59 through rolling countryside to the outskirts of Tuscaloosa, where the gleaming white plant is located, the famous Mercedes three-pointed star mounted on top of an obelisk out front. Ultrahip baby boomer CEO Andreas Renschler likes to call the place a "melting pot." But there is less evidence of melting than there is of fusion: various concepts have been brought together to create something new, but they still retain their distinction. Here at Vance, Mercedes has collected the technical expertise of its German engineering-focused culture, the willingness of its American workforce, and the careful attention to waste and detail that the best Japanese companies can boast. Inside Mercedes, Vance is known as a *lernfeld*—learning field.

Given the rare opportunity of a "clean sheet of paper" approach, Renschler began by building a team far different than any other Mercedes management group. He hired Bill Taylor from Toyota's Canadian plant in Cambridge, Ontario, as his vice president of operations. Inventory Manager Archie Craft came from Toyota's Georgetown, Kentucky, complex. Purchasing Vice President Bob Birch came from Nissan's sprawling complex in Smyrna, Tennessee. From Mercedes's giant Sindelfingen, Germany, plant, Renschler picked plant manager Hans-Joachim Schoepf and assembly trainers Michael Roeser and Harald Bosch. The idea was to draw from each manager's experience to create a new system.

Yet once meetings began, cultural clashes became the norm. Fundamental issues, like the configuration of the final assembly line, became monumental battles, not helped by the fact that the Mercedes managers would converse with each other in German after meetings, leading English-only speakers to wonder what decisions were being made without their input.[2] German managers expressed frustration with their North American counterparts' tendancy to openly discuss the pros and cons of every alternative. They were used to choosing a work method and getting on with it.

The wrangling might have continued indefinitely except that the team was facing rigidly set series of deadlines. There simply wasn't much time to fight. When it broke ground in Alabama in May 1994, Mercedes already had finished the first M-class prototypes. The company began hiring the first of its assembly workers in August 1994. Responses to advertisements in 10 local newspapers gave the first indication of the wide field of potential candidates from which Mercedes would choose. More than 45,000 people applied for the first 800 jobs, not quite the deluge that Toyota had encountered at Georgetown but certainly enough to give Mercedes encouragement. Like Toyota, Mercedes made use of assessment programs that helped identify workers who were open to new ideas, who were comfortable working in teams, and who could physically handle the work. In the assessment tests, the company was looking not just for speed but for people who could follow orders.

Begun without a union, the Alabama plant had just two job classifications, assembler and maintenance worker. The pay rate for both was $12.80 an hour, rising to more than $18.00 an hour after two years. That was roughly double the average hourly pay scale for manufacturing jobs across Alabama. But it was $6 an hour less than unionized workers at Detroit auto plants made, and more than $30 an hour less than the total compensation Mercedes paid its workers in Germany. Training began in April, 1995, when the first teams of Alabama workers went to Mercedes's sprawling Sindelfingen, Germany, plant to learn some basics about car building. Meanwhile, 70 specialists from Sindelfingen have been assigned to Alabama, for two-year stints to teach the fine points of Mercedes' craftsmanship to the new auto workers.

Mercedes officials hope the newcomers will have as much to teach the specialists as they will learn from them. Though Sindelfingen is home to Mercedes's flagship sedan, the $100,000-plus S-class, it is not by any stretch of the imagination one of the world's most efficient auto factories. It is an amalgamation of extensive automation, attempts at team-based work systems, and job shop, hand-built principles. Sitting on the edge of Stuttgart, Sindelfingen literally sprawls for miles, with 25,000 workers who make glass, steel, stampings, and plastic parts as well as automobiles. The visitors' center at the plant welcomes more than 20,000 customers a year who travel to Stuttgart by train to pick up their new cars. Some of them have placed their orders in the "Designo Center," a customization studio where buyers can select paint and leather interiors for their cars in colors ranging from copper to chartreuse and turquoise, a shock to the eyes of American consumers used to seeing Mercedes in only conservative blacks, navys, and silvers. Here, Mercedes executives dine in a starkly modern restaurant with gourmet food and fine wine that rivals any Stuttgart restaurant, while customers can hang out in a black-and-chrome decorated coffee shop that serves espresso and *apfel strudel*.

The busloads of visitors who come to Sindelfingen for tours every day probably don't notice that the concept of *takt* time is almost nonexistent on the assembly line. Whenever a quality glitch occurs on any Mercedes car, the line stalls while a swarm of Sindelfingen autoworkers, dressed in blue lab coats, surrounds it to find out the problem. Tour guides take special pride in pointing out Mercedes's army of robots, some of which do little more than move door panels from one side of an aisle to another. On what would normally be an interior trim line, Mercedes has assigned a squadron of Sindelfingen's elite craftsman, who are each given responsibility for making all the installations necessary to complete the car's interior. Armed with kits of shining tools, they individually work on their cars, like mechanics in a muffler repair shop. Though each has a series of assigned tasks, the steps are not mapped out, nor is each worker timed. When the work is done, the car is sent back to the final assembly line where teams of workers complete the production process.

It's a head-shaking process to anyone who is used to the stark efficiency of a Japanese automaker's factory. But the attention to detail has resulted in some of the world's finest cars and that is what Mercedes is striving to instill in its Alabama workers, while borrowing from the techniques that have led to Toyota's success. (The state of Alabama, which provided National Guard troops to clear the plant site, also picked up the $60 million bill for sending workers to Germany to train with the Sindelfingen *meisters*.)[3]

Surely no one in Sindelfingen would recognize the standardized method-and-procedure (SMP) charts found at every Vance workstation. These are Mercedes's version of the standardized work charts used by Toyota, which list the steps each worker must take to perform a task. Workers devised the steps in conjunction with managers, but they cannot be changed on the fly. The attention to detail is minute. On tables and pegboards near the assembly line, storage spots for wrenches and screwdrivers are marked off with tape, like chalk outlines police use for murder victims. If one of the Detroit automakers tried this, workers might respond by telling managers where they could stick the wrenches. At a Toyota plant, workers might quickly vote to eliminate the outlines as an excessive use of adhesive tape.

But here, since workers don't know that things aren't done this way elsewhere, the system was incorporated without protest. After all, anybody who landed a job here has already had to endure a lot of scrutiny, including a 32-hour preemployment skills test, part of the 80-hour screening procedure. Worker Charlene Paige says the directness in instructions is something that takes getting used to. "The Germans are very blunt and don't beat around the bush. You don't get politeness out of them about work. They're such perfectionists."[4] Conversely, the Mercedes officials express surprise at the touchy-feely approach they've found workers prefer. "They're not used to really open feedback. The Americans always want to hear that they're doing a good job," Renschler says.

Perhaps that is why Mercedes seems to be hedging its bets by beginning with a small workforce and a heavy reliance on its suppliers. About 20 percent of the M-class's parts come in preassembled modules. Where other plants have just-in-time inventory systems, Mercedes's system can best be called "just-in-sequence." Mercedes's 65 key suppliers all signed on to deliver the parts they make in the order in which Mercedes needs them. The plant's layout eases the way: It has only a body shop, paint shop and final assembly area. Parts are received at the body shop or at the final assembly area as they are required. For example, when an M-class body reaches the paint shop, an electronic message is sent via computer to a nearby Delphi Packard Electric plant. Delphi has 169 minutes to assemble and deliver a matching instrument panel, complete with gauges, controls, airbags, and the steering mechanism. Only two hours worth of parts are on the line, and a day's worth within the factory. There is no parts warehouse.[5] The supplier contracts are eight-year deals, twice as long as the typical Big Three U.S. automaker's contract, which generally runs the four-year life cycle of a vehicle. The longer Mercedes deals are typical in Europe, and also are intended to show Mercedes's dedication to long-term partnerships, a key factor in persuading suppliers to set up shop nearby.

Womack says that the arrangement also lessens the pressure on Mercedes, which is already under the gun in trying to build an all new vehicle with an all new workforce at an all new plant, a challenge that Big Three automakers regularly bobble. It took GM more than a year to bring its Lordstown, Ohio, assembly plant up to full speed in 1994 and 1995, when it began building Chevrolet Cavaliers with a smaller workforce and an all new manufacturing process. In its first month, the Lordstown plant built just 38 cars, less than half the number the plant would eventually build per hour. Mercedes did not expect to have nearly the problems that GM encountered, but it, too, was beginning with a slow production pace. Yet unlike the problem-plagued Cavaliers, early reviews of the M-class sport utilities were uniformly fantastic.

"There's nothing else out there that delivers such a refreshingly innovative blend of car-like handling and go-anywhere truck capabilities, glazed with luxury-sedan comfort and Mercedes cachet," raved James R. Healey of *USA Today*. Added *Car & Driver* magazine writer Fred Gregory, "The M-class inspires more confidence than Walter Cronkite, and I could think of no other sport (utility) in this class that could equal its handling." Ray Thursby of *European Car* stated that, "Mercedes has entered the sport-ute market with a machine that will rock the industry to its very foundation." Wrote Jean Lindamood Jennings of *Automobile* magazine, "The ML320, at about $35,000, is the Mercedes of sport utilities. We'd have one in a second."

None of the writers questioned whether Mercedes's move to Alabama had compromised the automaker's luxury car heritage. In fact, they did just the opposite—which was just what Mercedes executive Hubbert was striving for. "This company was focused for 11 years on Germany. Our marketing was 'Made in Germany.' We have to change it to 'Made by Mercedes.' We have to tell all of our markets that they can expect the same quality, the same durability," he says.

Success of the M-class is crucial not just for Mercedes's future in the sport utility market, but for its attempt to become a global manufacturer. Hubbert says the vehicle can inspire workers at Mercedes plants in Germany and a new plant under construction in Brazil to embrace the concepts that the company is using at Vance. Manager Andreas Roller, on loan from Sindelfingen, admits that he had trouble at first embracing the concept of standardized work: "Our feeling was, 'We already know how to build cars. This is like sending us back to kindergarten.' "[6] Now, Roller says he's come to view the tool as invaluable to teaching workers the fundamentals of building cars. Good thing he's changed his mind, because his job when he goes home is to teach Sindelfingen workers how to operate using standardized procedures.

If M-class weren't such a hit, changing the mind-set

of the veteran workers might be impossible. Says Hubbert, "That's why it's so important to have success in the marketplace. If everyone can see that it works, it works at other places, too. Everyone will be saying. 'Let's go, let's go.' The most difficult thing to do is to change their minds without products." Alabama assembly manager Archie Craft puts it more succinctly. "This operation has far more opportunity and potential to change an entire parent company than the Japanese transplants did," he says.

Womack thinks Mercedes is far from finished with its U.S. investment. He says the real breakthrough will come when Mercedes stops shipping German-made engines and transmissions to Alabama and announces plans for a U.S. engine plant. That's exactly what Japanese automakers did when they began building plants in the United States more than a decade ago. Says Womack: "For Mercedes, the important thing is to get the oceans out of the way."

Certainly, the opportunity to escape high labor costs and restrictive work rules and try new concepts made the United States attractive to a German company. But for proponents of the United States as a manufacturing base, no victory is sweeter than when a U.S. company decides to reinvest in a unionized factory in a traditional manufacturing location to make it competitive on a global scale. In the 1990s, one of the primary examples of a company rising from the ashes is Malden Mills in Lawrence, Massachusetts, which literally burned to the ground shortly before Christmas in 1995, to the horror of CEO Aaron Feuerstein and the company's 1,400 workers.

Feuerstein (pronounced "fewer-steen") has since become a corporate American folk hero for his decision to rebuild Malden Mills in Lawrence, which is 40 miles north of Boston, at a cost of $300 million. Nicknamed "the *mensch* of Malden Mills," Feuerstein, who is Jewish, has received two honorary degrees and been hosted at the White House. He sat next to First Lady Hillary Clinton at the 1996 State of the Union address and has been the subject of dozens of admiring profiles in publications such as *Reader's Digest, Parade* magazine, and the *Lands' End* catalog. Orders for Polartec, the patented lightweight fluffy fabric made from recycled soda bottles that Malden Mills produces, have skyrocketed, thanks to the publicity and the product's superior performance in ski, cycling, and sports attire. Malden Mills produces 900,000 yards of Polartec and Polarfleece a week. The fabrics, which represent 85 percent of Malden Mills's annual revenues, reached $400 million in sales in 1996 and soared to $500 million in 1997, up $125 million in less than two years.

Feuerstein is the first to wonder why he has gotten so much credit for doing something that felt right to him—and which was competitively correct. "Everything I did after the fire was in keeping with the ethical standards I've tried to maintain my entire life," Feuerstein says.[7] "Whether I deserve it or not, I guess I became a symbol of what the average guy would like corporate America to do at a time when the American dream has been pretty badly injured."

Some business experts have quietly suggested that maybe Feuerstein isn't a model in the modern manufacturing world. His own accountants and close advisors told him he was crazy to rebuild the 90-year-old family-owned mill, in the heart of a crumbling New England town, when he could easily pick up the operation and move to the southern United States, Mexico, or Asia, where thousands of fabric makers have fled during the past two decades. Unlike most of his competition, Feuerstein had most of his manufacturing ventures in one regional area. Along with the Lawrence factory, he had mills in Bridgeton, Maine, and Hudson, New Hampshire, with only one foreign factory, in Germany.

Analysts argued that Feuerstein had already shown his generosity to his 1,400 displaced workers after the fire. Each received a $275 Christmas bonus, a Polartec jacket, and several months salary and health care benefits, gestures that cost an estimated $15 million. Feuerstein's own insurance company gave him grief over the decision not to scrap the crumbling buildings and move to a site where it is cheaper and easier to operate, although the two sides ultimately settled their dispute.

"It seems pretty clear that some people call Feuerstein a saint because they don't have the courage to call him a fool," wrote author Thomas Teal in *Fortune* magazine.

But Feuerstein, whose grandfather founded Malden Mills in 1906 in Malden, Massachusetts, is nothing if not a firmly determined businessman. The true advantage of staying in Lawrence is not one of cost or even good publicity. It is the best move he could make to ensure product quality, satisfy customers, and ultimately earn Malden Mills higher profits. "Why would I go to Thailand to bring the cost lower when I might run the risk of losing the advantage I've got, which is superior quality?" Feuerstein asks. Quality was the reason that Feuerstein moved Malden Mills to Lawrence in 1956. He wanted to take advantage of the area's skilled craftsmen, such as textile designers, engineers, and assembly line workers who could give him an edge over other companies that had fled the region after World War II.

Even before it was placed in the spotlight by the

Toyota's outspoken president, Hiroshi Okuda, is pushing the Japanese auto giant to become more nimble and react faster to global trends. Even so, he admits Toyota is the world's best manufacturer.

Toyota Motor Manufacturing North America President Mikio "Mike" Kitano (shown with the Toyota Camry) and Toyota Motor Manufacturing Canada President Hiroake "Andy" Wantanabe have both been important players in Toyota's global push. Kitano is a leading student of the Toyota Production System, while Wantanabe had a hand in selecting the sites for every new Toyota plant in the late 1990s.

The Toyota Sienna (above) marks Toyota's attempt to compete in a key market dominated by the Big Three U.S. automakers. It is also a manufacturing challenge.
Workers in Georgetown, Kentucky (below), are building Siennas in the same plant
with Toyota Camry and Avalon sedans. Toyota uses a detailed assessment program to
select the best candidates for its assembly jobs.

Toyota's Georgetown, Kentucky, complex has grown from a car plant to a sprawling manufacturing center making engines, transmissions, and plastic components as well as cars and minivans. It is Toyota's biggest investment outside Japan.

Dana CEO Woodrow "Woody" Morcott is the driving force behind the largest U.S. auto supplier. Morcott's people-focused style has been critical to Dana's global success.

Dana President Joseph Magliochetti (left) and CFO Jack Simpson (below) are two key players in the company's global quest.

Two of Dana's sector presidents—Latin America's Chedo Eterovic (right) and Europe's Gus Franklin (below).

Chrysler CEO Robert Eaton (left) walks through Chrysler's plant in Cordoba, Argentina, in spring 1997. Eaton has crafted a careful expansion plan for Chrysler's international operations.

Chrysler Executive Vice President Dennis Pawley (right), the father of the Chrysler Operating System, is considered one of the U.S. auto industry's top manufacturing experts. Don Manvel (below) ran Chrysler's groundbreaking venture in Graz, Austria, and is now in charge of its Venezuelan operations.

Cummins CEO James Henderson (left) and President Tim Solso were the brains behind the Columbus, Indiana, engine maker's comeback and are the strategists of its joint-venture approach to global markets.

Cummins's union members showed their respect for legendary Cummins Chairman J. Irwin Miller (right) in 1997 by making him an honorary member of the Dieselworkers Union of America. Miller and Cummins Executive Vice President F. Joseph Loughrey (below) played crucial roles in convincing the DWU to reach an 11-year contract that has brought Cummins unprecedented labor peace.

The Mercedes M-Class sport utility breaks new ground for Germany's top luxury-car maker, both in manufacturing and in the auto market. By early 1998, less than six months after its debut, it had become the hottest thing on wheels in the U.S. market.

Mercedes workers Angelia Smith (above left) and Ronald Carter (above right) align the front bumper on an M-Class vehicle inside the Vance, Alabama, plant. Meanwhile, Mark Anders (below) installs a front seat. Made by Johnson Controls, the seats are delivered to Mercedes just minutes before they are to be installed.

A dramatic, nighttime view of the Mercedes visitors center, first stop for many who tour the Vance, Alabama, plant. The visitors center's design was recognized in 1997 by the American Institute of Architects. It has already become one of Alabama's top tourist attractions.

Mercedes board member Jürgen Hubbert, now in charge of the company's worldwide automotive operations. Hubbert was part of a team of executives who felt Mercedes' stodgy image had to change. He helped spur the M-Class project.

General Motors Corp. Chairman and CEO Jack Smith is pushing the world's biggest automaker to become a global standout. Yet GM's sales and labor problems in its home market could keep it from achieving all Smith hopes.

fire, Malden Mills was already a global competitor. Begun by Feuerstein's grandfather, Henry, as a maker of wool sweaters, by the late 1990s the company had grown to the world's largest producer of velvet upholstery and the largest exporter in the United States of high-performance fabrics like Polartec and Polarfleece. Until the market disappeared in the 1980s, Malden Mills also produced fake fur. Despite its New England location, exports are now one-third of its annual business, and it sells its products in 45 countries, with expansion underway in Asia and the Far East. Feuerstein opened a new European headquarters in fall 1997, in Maastrict, The Netherlands. It offers more than 200 patterns a year in 1,400 color combinations, and can make runs as small as 500 yards, a fraction of what most fabric producers usually require. The Polartec line was recently expanded to feature plaids and ribbing, along with conventional colored fleece.

With such diversity comes incredible customer loyalty. Malden Mills's customer retention rate is 95 percent, among the world's best. Its employee retention rate is about 95 percent, as good as any manufacturer can hope, given normal attrition rates of 3 to 4 percent nationwide. Between 1982 and 1995, Malden Mills's revenues tripled while the size of its workforce barely doubled—a sharp contrast to the United States's overall productivity increase of about 1 percent a year. Even before the fire, the company had already embraced computer-aided design and manufacturing equipment. It spends $20 million a year on new textile producing machinery. Its latest investment was equipment to make fashionable jacquard velvets, like the "burnout" fabric in vogue in late 1997.

The fire thus served as an opportunity for Malden Mills to become even more globally competitive. Even before the terrible December day when Feuerstein arrived at his manufacturing complex to find three buildings in flames, he had already authorized a $15 million overhaul of the company's information and automation systems. The fire destroyed half of Malden Mills's fiber-optic loop, wiped out half the telephones, destroyed about 300 personal computers, 160 printers, and all or part of 300 large dye and finishing machines.[8] Research and development studios lost formulas and designs for printing fabric. Some data was recovered, thanks to users who had taken diskettes home.

Instead of assigning the information systems rebuilding job to a computer specialist, Feuerstein chose Michael Backler, the company's director of planning and operations. Backler immediately stepped up implementation of a project called Merrimack, designed to shift Malden Mills to just-in-time inventory systems. Based on Malden Mills's research of best practices among the world's textile makers, the company now is aiming to manufacture each customer's order almost as soon as it is placed, instead of producing an inventory bank of fabric that is stored at Malden Mills's expense. Before, custom orders took at least two weeks and often four or five weeks to deliver. Now, Malden Mills is striving to deliver within days. It can now take orders on-line. "It was really designed to bring Malden Mills into the twenty-first century," says Malden Mills's spokeswoman Jennifer Summers.

There was one change mandated by the shift to the new $100 million facility: In order to concentrate on producing Polartec, Malden Mills was forced to cutback production of flocked velvet, used in furniture and wallpaper. For Feuerstein, that turned out to be another business no-brainer. Though it was a $120 million business, flocked velvet wasn't very profitable: It sells for just $3 a yard wholesale compared with an average of $8 a yard for Polartec. However, Feuerstein is hedging his bets, just in case yuppie hikers and Generation-X extreme-sports enthusiasts someday turn their backs on Polartec. He's keeping a research team working on flock, prepared to serve customers who can't live without that faux funeral parlor look for their sofas and walls.

The new technology that Malden Mills is using in its new factory requires about 400 fewer people than the 1,400 it employed in Lawrence before the fire. The unneeded workers are getting training for new jobs and some are taking their chances on returning to Malden Mills someday. Surprisingly, perhaps, Feuerstein isn't making any excuses for the downsizing. While his goal is to grow fast enough to employ the entire workforce, he is in favor of "legitimate downsizing, as the result of technological advances or good industrial engineering . . . We do it here all day long. We try to do it in such a way to minimize human suffering, but downsizing must be done." The trick, he says, is to focus on cutting waste, not simply to eliminate jobs (or, as GM calls its hourly workers, "Social Security numbers.") If a company's true motivation is simply to eliminate people, "That sort of thing is resented by labor, and you're never forgiven," Feuerstein says.

Some in the business world may never forgive Feuerstein for sticking to his principles. But author Womack suggests that his tactics, a combination of smart business management and a genuine desire to do good, may benefit the United States in its competitive quest against the rest of the world.

Says Womack, "Absolutely, this is a competitive place to do business. If we would just get our butts in gear, I would guarantee a happy ending." Like the one that Feuerstein has seen rise from the ashes.

6

The New Workforce

On a winding Kentucky country road off of I-75, past the McDonald's and the Shoney's Big Boy, beyond a black barn next to an old rambling white house where horses graze outside, sits a nondescript one-story building that few visitors to this glorious countryside would even notice. Dawn hasn't even broken on a gloomy late-spring morning, but already the spaces on the paved portion of the parking lot outside the Toyota Assessment Center have filled up. Anxious looking men and women, most in their 20s and 30s, clad in T-shirts, oxford-cloth button-downs, jeans, or jogging pants, are taking the last drags on cigarettes and filing through the center entrance. All are here for one reason: to land a job at one of Toyota's plants in its sprawling Georgetown, Kentucky, manufacturing complex. Today, for the first time ever, a visitor is joining them in the day-long assessment process that Toyota calls a Day of Work.

Ten years ago this building did not exist, while the concept behind it was still viewed with skepticism in traditional manufacturing circles. Well into the 1980s, many of the world's manufacturers thought of hourly workers as merely brawn, not a potentially valuable asset. Labor was seen as a variable cost to be adjusted according to the economic cycle, and it could be a downright nuisance in the case of an entrenched labor union. Job security was nonexistent: companies hired workers when times were good and laid workers off when times were bad. There was no need to assess candidates' qualifications: All anyone needed to land an assembly plant job was a high school diploma, and sometimes not even that. From the inner city neighborhoods of Detroit to the suburbs of Pittsburgh and the towns on the outskirts of Atlanta, generations of high school students found plentiful summer work in factories and steel mills, often toiling alongside parents, uncles, and even grandparents.

True, it was dirty, noisy, and sweaty working in a plant without air conditioning, especially in August heat. But how could a job at a department store paying $3.50 an hour, or a $9-an-hour checkout job at a Kroger grocery, compete with a temporary stint on the line paying $12 an hour? There was no need to wait while a manager checked your references: Show up to apply in the morning, and you could be working on the line that afternoon.

"From the late 60s to the 1980s, anybody standing and breathing could get a job," says St. John's University Labor Law Professor David Gregory. Often times, the pay that these jobs offered was too attractive to abandon when the summer ended. Generations of mothers and fathers who spent their own lives inside factories were distraught to see their youngsters follow in their footsteps. But the young people bet that the money they made in hourly pay and overtime could see them through an economic downturn that might throw them out on the street anyway from a lower-paying white collar job. Hundreds of thousands of people found out their bet was wrong in the 1980s, when industrial companies in the world's developed nations were hit simultaneously by a wicked recession and drastic corporate streamlining. When the companies finally weathered the storm, in the mid-1980s, they found that the manufacturing playing field was different.

Beginning with Japanese automakers' transplant operations in the United States and Europe, the hiring procedure for what had been blue-collar jobs became as thorough as the process for selecting management trainees. Technological advances on the factory floor, coupled with countless hours of study on how to build products more efficiently, have resulted in lean factories that require as few as one-third the workers that plants used to employ. The responsibilities that this smaller workforce bears are far greater than the few tasks their uncles, fathers, and grandfathers were asked to perform. Now, virtually all of the world's major manufacturers, from Volkswagen in Resende, Brazil, to Opel in Eisenach, Germany, are demanding that new applicants submit themselves to tests intended to prove their physical stamina, mental dexterity, and ability to solve problems alone and in groups.

Those who succeed have joined an elite society of new-collar workers, making administrative, engineering, manufacturing, and even marketing decisions that rival the kinds of responsibilities that traditionally fell only to college-educated management employees several levels above workers on the factory floor in the chain of command. For the companies, finding these candidates is a time-consuming and expensive proposition. And nowhere is it more extensive than at Toyota, leader among the Global Manufacturing Vanguard in the precision with which it assesses the people who seek to become its new collar workers.

Toyota estimates it spends $3,000 for each job applicant who makes it all the way through the selection process and gets a job at one of its factories, and thousands of dollars more on training after a job candidate is hired. Yet according to Professor Gregory, "In light of what these people are being asked to do, $3,000 that isn't all that much in the long term." For the applicants, the expense, scrutiny, and competition make the chances of being hired slim. Since it began building cars at Georgetown in 1986, Toyota has received more than 200,000 applications from across Kentucky and throughout the United States. Toyota originally hired 2,000 people. But, in subsequent years, Toyota has expanded to 7,500 employees at two car assembly plants and an engine and transmission factory.

Yet the expansion has not lowered Toyota's standards. In the first half of 1997, Toyota was striving to hire an additional 350 people at Plant No. 2, which was about to become the first in North America to build cars and minivans on the same line—Camry, the best-selling car in the United States, and the new Sienna minivan, to be introduced in fall 1998. By July, about 900 applicants had gone through interviews and an initial written test that led them to the 12-hour Day of Work, the most extensive portion of the job interview process, conducted at the Assessment Center. Yet, only 100 of those people landed jobs and Toyota faced the prospect of ending the year short of the number of hires it hoped to make.

Never before has Toyota allowed a journalist to participate in the assessment process. Public relations representative Barbara McDaniel joins me as the Day of Work begins at 6:30 A.M. The tense applicants are in their seats as assessor Bill Kinney greets them and pops a cassette into a video player. This is the first of four groups of six people each who will sit in these folding chairs today. Toyota holds the assessment sessions six days a week. Wearing name tags bearing their first names—Chris, Stacey, Jesse,—the applicants gaze intently at the screen, which outlines what they can expect to experience throughout the day. They are told they must don safety glasses, hard hats, gloves, and sleeve protectors while they are working on Toyota's mock assembly line. They cannot smoke except during two 15-minute breaks and one 45-minute lunch break. If anyone is injured, he or she must immediately tell an instructor and cannot leave the building before help arrives.

Flipping off the VCR, Kinney tells the applicants that now is the time to leave if anyone feels unable to perform the day's routine. "We want you to be at your best," he says. Leaving does not eliminate applicants from the job pool: They will get another chance to go through the Day of Work in six months. Some of the people here are on their third try, Kinney confides. Assessor Fern Edgett says it isn't uncommon for applicants to disappear during the day. "We always lose a bunch at lunchtime," she says. One time an applicant asked for permission to go to the ladies' room. All that was ever seen of her again was her name tag, left by the sink. Toyota prefers that doubters excuse themselves, Edgett says. "We aren't doing them a favor if we give them a job and they can't handle it."

This morning, everybody stays put. The video is followed by a 10-minute series of stretches that prompt some uncomfortable giggles from the job seekers. "Good morning—*Ohio Goziamus*," a soothing instructor's voice chirps from a boom box as the prospective autoworkers reach their arms into the air and bend down to their toes. The mini-aerobics session is the only comic relief that these people will have for the next four hours. This first group is starting with the most difficult part of the assessment program: four hours on a pair of simulated assembly lines, designed to weed out candidates who simply do not have the physical stamina or mental attitude to handle the repetitive tasks that autoworkers must perform.

The first task is dubbed Rim Mount and seems ridiculously simple. It involves unbolting and rebolting wheel rims mounted in three rows on a large piece of particle board propped behind a work station on the simulated assembly line. Yellow tape at the candidates' feet marks off where the line would begin. As will be discovered with each of the exercises on the day's agenda, however, Rim Mount is hardly as easy as it appears. Kinney hands each candidate a black binder with instructions on how to perform the job. He tells them they must follow the steps in order, and walks them through the routine in aching detail. "You might see a better way. You can't use that better way," he warns them. No one on the asssessment staff mentions that the applicants' ability to follow these steps unquestioningly will be a key factor in determining whether they have the aptitude to learn the Toyota Production System.

The candidates are soon decked out in protective garb—hard hats, gloves, glasses, earplugs, aprons, and wrist bands—and in position on their work station platforms, where each will carry out the designated task. They are told to pick up their yellow air guns with their right hands; for some it is the first time they have ever held a pneumatic tool. Kinney proceeds to instruct them in how to unbolt the first rim and they follow along, using their air guns to unscrew every other lug nut so the rim remains balanced; sorting the nuts by color into the pockets of their aprons; and replacing their air guns into the holsters provided. They are then told to remove the unbolted wheel cover and place it on a rack behind their work stations on the correct shelf—A, B, or C—arranged by wheel cover weight. Next, they must check a manifest hanging by the side of their work stations for the type of wheel cover that will replace the one just removed. They must then return to the rack, grasp the correct wheel cover with two hands, climb back onto the platform, and begin bolting on the new wheel cover, being careful to mount it with its air valve hole in the right place. Kinney tells them the cover will stay in place better if the bottom lug nut is manually screwed on first, followed by one at the opposite corner. He wants them to screw in every other nut until all are in place. After that, the nuts are torqued with the air gun. They finish by checking manually to make sure the nuts are screwed on tight, and then replacing the air guns in their holster. Finally, they step down off the platform and draw a pencil line through the wheel cover that has just been replaced.

The group gets three practice tries as Kinney offers critique. At 7:45 A.M., he says, "Okay, you've got two hours. Give it your very best effort." Now the group is in the hands of Don Dykman, a lanky man with kind eyes. Armed with a clipboard, he is keeping watch for any variation from the prescribed methodology.

Lug nuts fall to the ground from one applicant's nervous fingers. Dykman instructs the individual to pick up the nuts immediately. Toyota does not tolerate untidy work stations. Quickly fatigued, applicants find it most difficult to attach and remove the lower three wheel mounts, which hang close to the simulated assembly line floor. It is tempting to sit down on the platform to get at them comfortably, but Dykman rules that out: workers must squat or kneel. It is difficult to build speed early on because the lug nuts seem very much alike. The only difference between some is a thin band of copper or gold around the inside edge. But each type is meant to support a different weight of wheel cover. An incorrect lug nut will not tighten correctly.

Plastic safety glasses begin to fog up, hard hats slip off sweaty foreheads, and applicants unused to repetitive work find their tight muscles sore after just a few minutes. It's easy to spot improvements that could be made in the manufacturing process. One applicant asks Dykman why she must remove a wheel cover, place it on the rack, come back to check the manifest, then go back for the wheel cover. Wouldn't it be simpler to check the manifest on the way to the rack? That way, she could pick up the next wheel cover when she drops off the previous one. Dykman nods, but tells her to simply make a mental note. This is the kind of issue that would require discussion by other members of a work team, to see if all wanted to operate that way.

The Rim Mount exercise complete, applicants move immediately to the other side of the room. Now comes another easy-at-first-glance activity. Edgett tells each group member to pick up two perforated metal plates. Each pair of plates attaches to a clip on an adjustable metal arm. Applicants are to spend the next two hours selecting tiny nuts and bolts from nearby bins in order to screw the two plates together with a screwdriver.

When they've done that, they're to unscrew each set of nuts and bolts, remove the plates from the clip, sort the nuts and bolts back into the bins, and then move to clip to a different height on the metal arm. The exercise requires them to perform the assembly and disassembly at three different heights: above their heads, at waist level, and near their knees.

Edgett, making notes, says she is looking for accuracy, tempo, and the ability to follow procedure. This exercise doesn't involve the heavy equipment that Rim Mount required, but it is far more tedious. Nuts and bolts fall to the floor with pinging sounds as they slip from tired hands. Arms become even more sore because applicants are stretching over their heads to attach and unscrew. Legs ache even more from squatting once again to perform the tasks. Where Rim Mount required physical stamina, this exercise requires deftness with an easy-to-drop screwdriver, and much more concentration to make sure nuts and bolts go into the correct bins. Where Rim Mount was punctuated by the whir of air guns, this activity is done mostly in silence, except for an occasional sign of frustration.

When the four hours of simulated manufacturing are complete, applicants pour out of the room, all sweating, some swearing, and head for a quick gulp of water, a fast Coke, or a drag on a cigarette during a precious 15-minute break. But they can't relax because they must remain on their feet for another hour. In the final exercise of the morning, they are taken to a classroom where they find shelves full of colorful bundles wrapped in red, blue, yellow, and black felt, each crisscrossed with ties. This is Inspection, and inside the bundles are stacks of thin steel plates. Standing behind counters, wearing work gloves, the applicants are to scrutinize each plate for defects, such as a scratch, an incorrectly drilled hole, pitting, or perforations. Some of the plates might have more than one defect. The applicants are to note the number and type of defects on score sheets.

Each shelf is stacked with three bundles of 12 plates each. Applicants will get eight minutes to inspect as many as they can. They are told to keep their work stations neat, and to carefully retie the bundles when they are through because they will be judged on precision.

Edgett, on hand again (assessors typically travel with group members through three exercises), says the exercise is meant to determine who has the eagle eyes needed to spot problems on the assembly line. Toyota has eliminated the hundreds of inspectors still on hand in Big Three U.S. automakers' factories. Instead, it is up to Toyota workers to find defects, make note of them, and see what kind of changes should be made to correct them. A car comes off the Georgetown assembly line every 55 seconds, Edgett notes. Edgett notes that while the applicant's have eight minutes for their inspection, "our team members only have 55 seconds."

Yet even those eight minutes seem short this morning. The room's fluorescent light makes it hard to spot some problems and slows some applicants down. No one makes it through more than two bundles during any of the four eight-minute inspection stretches. Once time runs out, Edgett prowls the room for suggestions: What kinds of defects were most prevalent? Did some bundles have fewer defects than others? How could the job been made easier? She is trying to find out who has paid the closest attention to patterns that could indicate a problem with a batch of parts on the assembly line.

The most physically demanding part of the day is now over, and some applicants' fates are already sealed. During the day, applicants will receive two

scores—one for the assembly and inspection phase, another for the upcoming series of teamwork and analytical exercises. Publicly, Toyota and other manufacturers stress the importance placed on strong intellectual and social skills. But Edgett says that the production portion carries the most weight here. "If you don't pass production, your other scores don't make up for it," she explains. However, a mediocre production score could be shored up with a strong intellectual score. And vice-versa: Someone who has doubtful interpersonal skills might land a job if he or she is a standout on the simulated assembly line.

Ideally, however, Toyota wants a combination of both, which is why applicants will spend the rest of the day in classrooms. First comes a written test, Toyota's version of a Harvard Business School case study text. They are handed a scenario about a crisis on the assembly line: It seems that since the factory changed over to production of new models, defects are up and customers are getting angry. Inside the plant, morale is plummeting, the air conditioning system has broken, and injuries are increasing. The case comes with pages of Statistical Process Control (SPC) charts showing the running rate of defects on the cars, and measuring where in the plant workers are the most unhappy. There are also eight memos from autoworkers detailing their complaints. Among them: "The procedures that worked before seem really cumbersome since the model change." "After doing the same task all day, boredom is really a problem." "It's just too hot to work in there." "The parts are not there when you need them." "I can't always find the crowbar I need to do this."

Using the complaints and statistics, each applicant is asked to diagnose the assembly line problems and write recommendations for fixing them. It's a challenge for anybody schooled in manufacturing process, let alone a job applicant who may have never set foot in a plant. But Edgett says Toyota isn't looking for sophisticated analyses. It is trying to see who can size up a situation, find the root cause of the problem, and come up with ideas that address the issues involved. These are just the kind of challenges that team members face every day at Georgetown, she says. "A lot of this is analytical and a lot of it is communication," she adds.

The crisis assessment exercise is the last the applicants perform alone. Next the six job seekers huddle around a classroom table, listening anxiously as assessor Laurie Bond gives them instructions. The group has become a supplier of electrical circuit boards to mythical B&B Electronics. During the next two hours, they will assemble circuit boards and sell them to B&B, buying their first set of parts with $25 in seed money. Five different types of circuit boards are laid out on a table behind them, complete with a list of parts needed, the price for the raw materials, and the price the boards will bring from B&B. The group members can inspect the boards, but they cannot take them back to the table and copy their construction. The boards range from cheap and easy to assemble, but yielding little profit, to expensive and complicated to assemble, with a high profit margin. The $25 will pay for just one of the expensive boards, but a number of cheap ones.

The exercise is divided into discussion and production periods. During discussion, group members hash out which boards they want to build and make notes on the parts they will need. When production begins, they must go to a nearby B&B cashier, played by an assessor, to order parts for their boards; build the boards; complete necessary paperwork listing their asking price; sell the boards; and purchase parts for new ones. Everything must fit perfectly, or the cashier can reject the parts without giving a reason why. Bond is watching the group as they interact: Who takes charge as leader? Who has the best memory for the parts that are needed? Who has strong financial skills?

Quickly a feisty blonde woman named Susan begins drilling her five male colleagues on their preferences. She suggests buying midpriced components so the group can earn a reasonable profit but not sweat over intricate production. The group, whose members include two nearly silent participants, follows her lead. Parts are purchased, the scramble to assemble them begins, and Susan quickly tallies up what the board should bring. She walks it over to the cashier, who scans the board and order sheet. "I can't accept it," Susan is told.

That sets off a mad scramble for reasons why: Are the parts correctly connected? Are there enough clips and diodes? The group makes some adjustments to the board and Susan returns to the cashier, only to be rejected again. And again; five times in all. By now, the group is puzzled, yet no one loses his or her temper, no one yells, no one points fingers. As time runs out, they find out what went wrong: their paperwork. Susan throws her hands in the air. "Man!" she exclaims as the others laugh. It's a much calmer reaction than Edgett has come to expect. Circuit boards have been thrown against blackboards or slammed on table tops. Once, she had to break up a fight between two candidates.

"You put them under pressure and you see their behavior. This really brings out their personalities," Edgett says. Though Susan may have seemed overly brash in her take-charge attitude, Edgett explains she was actually pleased to see her show leadership skills.

Susan may have had some coaching: Her husband is a team member at the Georgetown plant and Edgett surmises he probably briefed his wife on the traits she should show during the exercise.

The final exercise of the day, Personal Touch, is fun: Because they achieved quality goals the previous month, Toyota is giving each member of the work team $9 to spend on a reward. The group is handed a list of options, ranging from pizza every Friday for a month, at $6 a person, to an outing at King's Island amusement park, for $30 a person. If they choose the trip, they must come up with the extra $21 themselves, and families cannot accompany them. The group, like a jury, must reach a unanimous decision on what the reward will be. This team quickly spots a compromise: a trip to the Kentucky State Fair, which will cost $9 each, including spouses and children. The group writes up its recommendation and hands it in. The Day of Work is complete.

But the assessment process is not. For a lucky handful, the Day of Work is followed by an in-depth job interview. Early the next morning, assessor Tom Stubblefield, wearing a natty suit instead of the work clothes he donned at the center the day before, sits at a table in a small conference room at the Georgetown plant. Across from him sits Jo Williams, 30, who excelled on a Day of Work the previous month. A high school graduate, Williams has spent the intervening years in a series of blue-collar jobs. She has shown the stamina and thinking ability to fit in well at Toyota, and Stubblefield is excited about talking with her.

Yet Williams is more subdued than confident as she listens to Stubblefield explain that Toyota currently is hiring only entry-level assembly workers. Williams's shift would be 5:30 P.M. to 2:15 A.M., and she would usually be able to expect overtime. "The work is fast, the pace is monotonous and repetitive," Stubblefield warns her. But Williams says that this would be fine.

The reason why quickly becomes clear. Williams is currently working two jobs five days at week. One is at Black & Decker's nearby Lexington, Kentucky, plant, and the other is for United Parcel Service (UPS) at Lexington's airport. She arrives for her Black & Decker job at 3 P.M., working until 11 P.M., and then proceeds to her 2 A.M. to 6 A.M. stint at UPS. Clad in blue jeans, she has come to this 8 A.M. interview directly from her UPS job, where she "loads bellies" of airplanes. Together, the two jobs pay her about $14 an hour for 15 hours work—about $4 an hour less than the $18 she would make at Toyota, working just a single eight-hour shift.

Stubblefield prods Williams into describing a typical work day. At Black & Decker (B&D), Williams explains, she hones the edges of saw blades used in various types of power tools. She operates three machines simultaneously, each cutting a stack of blades at a time. "How many blades a day is that?" Stubblefield asks. At least 12,000, Williams says as Stubblefield's eyes widen. "That's a lot," he replies. At UPS, Williams continues, she is the only person trained on her shift to handle a freight-loading forklift, whose complicated controls she likens to a Nintendo game. With just 15 minutes to unload and load an aircraft, any mistake by the freight loader can delay a takeoff. "Maybe that's why nobody else wants to do it," she muses. Openly impressed, Stubblefield asks her if she's ever made any suggestions on her jobs that led to quality or process improvements. It's hard for Williams to come up with any. But then she remembers that at one previous job she had worked closely with engineers to improve an assembly line task. The outcome led to her assignment as an engineering trainee, rare for an assembly line worker with no college experience.

Williams stops, embarrassed. "I'm making it sound like something earth-shattering," she says. Stubblefield shakes his head, encouraging her to continue. As Williams talks, he sees on her job application that she left the company soon after she was made an engineering trainee. Williams explains she was laid off in a wave of corporate cutbacks. Her hoped-for promotion to a management job never came through, forcing her back into a blue-collar job. The discussion seems to have opened an old wound for Williams, and Stubblefield senses it's time for a break. "I hope this hasn't seemed like an inquisition," he says, pointing her toward the ladies' room. When she is gone, he smiles broadly. "When they're good [candidates], they just jump out at you," he says. He's sure that Toyota's training system, in time, will bring out Williams's leadership ability on the factory floor and improve her self-confidence.

Upon Williams's return, Stubblefield gives her a brochure about the Georgetown plant, explains that drug screening is required of all prospective hires, and promises Toyota will get back to her soon. He tells her it may be a month before she gets an offer—and probably three more months before she sets foot on a factory floor.[1] In the meantime, Williams would be asked to go through more time on a simulated assembly line, take classes in Toyota's manufacturing process and philosophy, and attend a daily aerobics workout designed to build strength. None of it would be a problem, Williams assures Stubblefield. For the first time that morning, she looks visibly pleased.

Hard as it might be for Georgetown applicants like Williams to imagine, Toyota was about to make its application process tougher. As Williams was interviewing for a job, Toyota was finishing the roof on its 1.2 million square foot truck plant in Princeton, Indiana, about two hours away from Georgetown. The company plans to open the factory in fall 1998 to build 100,000 T-150 pickup trucks a year with just 1,100 workers. By contrast, a General Motors (GM) truck plant might employ five times as many workers. But Toyota plans to give its Princeton workers even more responsibility on the assembly line than even Georgetown's workers enjoy. As such, they can expect to go through additional assessment tests, including more problem-solving and teamwork exercises.

"We will start with a very lean organization," promises Seizo Okamoto, Toyota Motor Manufacturing Indiana President. "The individual has got to bear more responsibility." Seizo already knows what manufacturing workers are capable of achieving, even those from the old school. Before taking over the plant in Princeton, he was in charge of New United Motor Manufacturing Inc. (NUMMI), Toyota's joint car- and truck-building venture with GM in Fremont, California. In Fremont Toyota took on some of GM's most disgruntled workers, individuals who had lost their jobs in the early 1980s when GM closed their plant. The workforce had been rife with absenteeism and drug use prior to the plant's closing, but under the terms of its deal with GM, Toyota could not select its own workers until it used up the pool of unemployed plant veterans.

Yet by embracing Toyota's training methods and manufacturing system, the plant was transformed into a streamlined operation building top-quality vehicles. In 1997, the NUMMI plant scored best in initial customer satisfaction on an internal GM study of its car factories. It has won numerous awards from automotive marketer J. D. Power and Associates for product quality. And it is still visited weekly by other companies trying to find out the Toyota secret to motivating workers.

Okamoto openly expects the Princeton plant will become the latest stop on the Toyota manufacturing tour, as much for its people processes as for its manufacturing methods. He plans to create a force of "self-concluding workers," a concept new to Toyota. They will be able to make the kind of quick fixes and process changes that assessors at Georgetown warned applicants not to attempt for fear of upsetting the standardized work system. "Even team members can plan their own process, discover and solve problems," Okamoto says.

But to do so may require different types of skills than those that previous Toyota plants required. Thus Okamoto wants to hire workers ranging in age from their 20s to their late 40s. Some of the older individuals may be manufacturing veterans who understand factory flow better than younger colleagues coming straight from Indiana farms or small towns. One of the key players in finding these workers will be a GM veteran, co-plant manager Norm Bafunno. Before he came to Toyota, Bafunno was in charge of developing the manufacturing methods that will be used to build GMT800, GM's replacement for its aging Chevrolet C/K pickup, scheduled for introduction in 1998. Though GMT800 is an important truck for GM, and the manufacturing job a crucial one, Bafunno was frustrated by GM's slowness in getting the program going. By the time the pickup reaches the market, it will have been more than three years since Ford restyled its F-series pickup, the Chevy truck's closest competitor, and four years since Chrysler introduced the gutsy Dodge Ram.

"Somebody called me and said, 'Norm, would you

be interested?' And I thought, 'It's something to listen to. It's Toyota,' " Bafunno says, explaining his jump from GM to Toyota. (Bafunno's timing was superb. Just weeks after he joined Toyota, the United Auto Workers staged a three-month strike at GM's Pontiac, Michigan, truck plant and engineering complex.) Bafunno was attracted by the closeness with which managers were expected to work with Toyota's team members. Just 10 percent of Princeton's staff will be managers, compared with 16 percent at Georgetown and about 25 percent at traditional plants. Further, Toyota had no union to contend with at Georgetown or Princeton that might impede company progress.

"Our people understand what is at stake, and what will help us grow in the future," says Bafunno. "As our team members decide that something needs to be done, we can do it quickly."

Indeed, none of the Japanese or European automakers' plants in the United States, except NUMMI and Mitsubishi's factory in Normal, Illinois, once co-owned by Chrysler, are unionized. Together, foreign-owned auto plants employ almost 40,000 autoworkers who are not United Auto Workers (UAW) members. Analysts have long felt the hand-selection process has stymied the union's attempt to organize the factories. "Without a doubt, the assessment process is a competitive advantage," says Lehman Brothers Senior Vice President Joseph Phillippi. "First of all, you can deselect prounion people. And by not having a third party, you're not going to have the creation of work rules that get in the way of productivity improvements."

Yet Toyota has dealt successfully with unions in its home country, Japan, and in other nations, such as England and Brazil, where labor organizations are commonplace. And Vanguard member Cummins Engine has found that cooperation with a key union can play a major role in a company's global competitiveness.

Cummins's 1997 shareholders' meeting, held in its picturesque hometown of Columbus, Indiana, was poignant for many of the people who attended. It marked the retirement of longtime Chairman J. Irwin Miller from the Cummins board, on which he served from 1936 to 1997. More than just a businessman, Miller had been Cummins's heart and soul, and the city of Columbus's as well. It was Miller, educated at Yale and Oxford, who convinced some of the world's most famous architects to build some of their masterpieces in this small city whose population of 37,000 is well outnumbered by the architecture buffs who descend upon it every year. Just a few blocks from Cummins's light-filled headquarters, designed by Kevin Roche and John Dinkeloo, stands Eero Saarinen's North Christian Church with its 192-foot spire, I. M. Pei's public library, and an elementary school conceived by Edward Larrabee Barnes. These eye-pleasing modern buildings are a vivid contrast to the older Victorian and Arts and Crafts-style structures of which the city is also proud. One of them, the elegant Irwin bank building, was built by Miller's ancestors early this century.

In the same way that he brought the architectural talent of the world to Columbus, it was Miller, the owner of a Stradivarius violin he calls "my fiddle," who put Cummins on the map as a global manufacturer, expanding the company's vision beyond its traditional U.S. base. The farewell of such an industrial notable was bound to be marked by effusive speeches; Miller's departure was. And sharing the spotlight with Cummins board member Franklin Thomas at Miller's farewell was Dieselworkers Union of America (DWU) President Conrad Dowling.

Clad in a white button-down work shirt, Dowling peered at a teleprompter on the podium as the stooped, white-haired Miller watched from a seat in the audience.

"While we were on opposite sides of the table, and we didn't always agree, there wasn't a day when we doubted your intentions or your respect for us as workers," Dowling said haltingly. "We always knew that you operated from a set of principles, values, and ethical standards that in the end, would bring all of us together." Dowling thanked Miller for a business vision that "brought all of us jobs so that we could live in comfort. You were at the top of the company, with lots of important strategic issues vying for your attention. Yet you always had time for those of us on the shop floor."

Dowling continued: "We could talk to you, and we knew you'd listen. You came to our gatherings, and we knew you cared." As a parting gift, Dowling unfurled the DWU flag signed by every member of the union. And he displayed a plaque, naming Miller an honorary lifetime member of the DWU. "This is perhaps unprecedented in the world of labor relations," Dowling continued over applause from shareholders who had jumped to their feet, some wiping tears from their eyes. "But you are unprecedented in the world of business leadership. And we could not think of a better way to honor you for all you have done for all of us." Union Secretary-Treasurer Rudy Baker, presenting Miller with the membership certificate, told him he could stop by the union hall for coffee and doughnuts any time.

"Free?" Miller asked. "You'll see me there." Embracing Dowling, who had walked to stand by his side, Miller said, "I can't think of anything I will treasure more than this."

But there had been no hugs or tears four years earlier

when the DWU and company officials were engaged in what was probably the toughest set of negotiations Cummins had ever seen. Even as it battled financial crises in the 1980s and early 1990s, the company had branched out, with plants in Brazil, Mexico, and Scotland producing the same engines that Cummins made in its main Columbus Engine plant, which was built in 1926. "They were making huge decisions about future investments. We were seeing a lot of products leave the area [for overseas plants,]" Dowling says.

This, plus the stiff competition posed by Komatsu and other foreign companies, frightened Cummins workers, whose ages averaged in their 40s. The plants' oldest workers were in their 50s, and all were well aware of the pressure being put on Cummins and other major U.S. companies. "This workforce is very knowledgeable about the global marketplace," says Dowling. The issues came up in an extraordinary set of negotiations that began the week before Christmas 1992, and stretched over four months.

At the first session, which included Miller, Cummins's top executives, and 70 union stewards, Cummins executive Joseph Loughrey hammered home the point that "if we weren't there already, we were drifting to uncompetitiveness. Whether the company made a conscious choice to move out or not, we weren't going to be here (in Indiana) anywhere like we were in the past. We made it a competitive issue. We were trying to make the case for why we had to do something really different."

Cummins wanted flexibility to make its processes cheaper and faster to complete. It saw how team-based work systems had improved efficiency at Toyota and at GM's Saturn plant. It had already implemented the idea at another plant, in Jamestown, New York, and had begun using it at nearby Cummins Mid-Range Engine Plant (CMEP). Now the company wanted to try the concept at Columbus.

Union members, seeing what a U.S. recession in the early 1990s had done to workers in other Midwest industrial towns, had their own priority: guaranteed jobs for the life of the contract. "We had people that had 19 years seniority that were still getting laid off. You can't plan your life if you've worked at a place for 19 years and you're still getting laid off," says former DWU President Larry Neihart, who led the union's bargaining team in the talks. "Ever since 1981, they'd been on us about getting some kind of employment security."

Neihart knew that the team-based work system idea would run into immediate resistance among many older workers, who were long set in their ways. But he did not want to turn the idea down before he talked about it with younger workers who had been assigned to CMEP. Some had subsequently returned to the main Columbus engine plant, where wages were higher. "I had some people tell me they liked the [CMEP] work system better than at Plant One. That started opening my eyes a little," Neihart says.

He could sense that the point was important to Loughrey. "I knew what the company wanted real bad. We wanted employment security and better retirement. It's always holding this carrot up. We were holding the carrot up to say, 'how much do you want this work system?' That's what negotiations are all about," he says.

The union agreed to try the team concept and then began addressing a point important to both sides. Cummins did not want to come back to the bargaining table three years hence, as was the standard industry practice. Company officials wanted to be able to make business plans into the next century. Doing so would necessitate a longer contract. The first proposal was five years. But then the two sides hit upon a breathtaking compromise: "What if we went 11 years?" Neihart suggested. That period would guarantee wages and benefits for every senior worker on Cummins's payroll. "We knew they wouldn't all retire, but they would be eligible," he explains.

Each year before its contracts were up, Cummins had been hit by a flock of retirements by workers afraid they would lose benefits through contract concessions during the next round of negotiations. As part of the 11-year agreement, believed to be among the longest of any U.S. labor union, Cummins was willing to increase cost-of-living allowances and retirement benefits every three years, as if a normal-length contract was in effect. Both sides seemed happy with the deal. But before negotiations could be wrapped up, they almost went into the ditch.

Under an accounting standard called FAS 106, U.S. corporations were required to estimate by the end of 1993 how much they would pay out over the coming decades in employee and retiree health care benefits. Cummins's estimate was a staggering $251 million, nearly four times its net income for 1992. The company ended up with an overall loss of $190 million for the year, and executives decided steps need to be taken to slice the cost of those future benefits. Early in 1993, Cummins decreed that current and future retirees would have to pay a greater portion of their health care benefits than retirees had in the past. The change affected every employee on the roster, from union members to CEO James Henderson.

Loughrey admits Cummins's timing of the announcement, during the contract talks, was dreadful.

"Rather than waiting until after we settled the agreement, then facing this big issue, we said, 'Even though this might shoot all our dreams, we are going to deal with it up front.' We said, "These are the changes we are going to make, these are the processes we are going to follow.' And they went basically berserk."

Negotiations immediately broke off. "There were a lot of things that we had to do that we had to search our guts to see if we were really ready to do [them]. It was a hostile situation [at] the table. I went up and said, 'we're leaving and we'll be back.' " Neihart recalls. Loughrey was deluged with more than 1,500 memos and letters from angry employees. Meanwhile, at the engine plant, many workers' first reaction was, "I wonder if Mr. Miller knows about this?" Over the years, Miller had been a frequent visitor to Cummins's plants. He knew many of the workers by name, knew the names of their wives and children and took note of his employees' accomplishments on the job and off. He was fond of saying that workers on the shop floor often understood more about Cummins's operations than its executives. Neihart had first gotten to know Miller years before, and the pair were on a first-name basis.

So Neihart called Miller at his vacation home in Florida to discuss the retiree benefit changes. "He said, 'Hello, Larry, how are you?' " Neihart recalls. Neihart unloaded his concerns on the Cummins Chairman, who was apologetic but told Neihart that Cummins was forced to take action. Other companies had cut retirees' benefits much more drastically than Cummins proposed. "I didn't like it, but he's the only guy who would explain it to me so that I would listen," Neihart says.

With the two sides still apart, Neihart took to walking the floors of Cummins's plants, trying to gauge the depth of workers' lingering anger. One day a worker called him over to ask about the progress of the talks. Word of the longer contract and Cummins's proposed work system had reached the shop floor. Neihart explained to the worker that it would be hard to give up the union's past gains (called "language" in labor movement terminology) in order to win the 11-year deal. "He looked at me and said, 'I'd like you to tell me one thing: What good does that language do me while I'm laid off? It's your job to make sure that I have a job. I have a wife and two kids and I'm able to work under any system this company throws at me. If you keep the language, what have you done for me?'"

Says Neihart, "I didn't sleep very much that night. I made up my mind that guy was going to have a job." Negotiations resumed two weeks later, and the two sides ultimately hammered out the 11-year contract. To help workers feel comfortable with the team concept, Cummins held seminars during the first few years of the contract to explain it, and did not fully implement it until 1996. Both sides say the contract has been like a marriage. "You have an ongoing partnership, and you talk about ongoing changes," Plant Manager Rich Freeland says. Adds Dowling, "Your expectations change. On any given day, there are peaks and valleys. You're high one day, you have problems the next." But instead of putting off those problems to a new round of negotiations, Dowling says the DWU and Cummins are forced to deal with issues as they arise.

Silver-haired Dowling, who retired in 1998, and preppy-looking Freeland regularly walked the plant floor together, clad in nearly identical golf shirts and slacks, to address workers' concerns and share information from management. Despite the growing pains of adjusting to a contract almost four times as long as a typical pact, Dowling says that no one wants to return to Cummins's previous mass production system. "I think 100 percent of them [workers] would say, 'Hell, no!' To try to change things now and go backward would be to tear down trust."

It would also wipe out demonstrable gains in workers' knowledge and productivity. Under the team-based system, now being used in five Cummins plants, each worker has received 64 hours of classroom instruction on problem solving and error detection, similar to the types of training Toyota workers undergo. Inside the plant, Cummins set up three assembly lines to practice new manufacturing techniques. By mid-1997, a year and a half into the system, the plant was producing 15 more engines per day than in 1993, using one-third less floor space and fewer workers. Cummins had eliminated two layers of plant management. Most important, it is investing $225 million to build another new engine, the Signature 600, at the Columbus plant. Aimed at winning more worldwide heavy-duty truck business, the engine will go into production in 1998.

Even with the gains, Dowling admits the 11-year agreement has drawn disdain from some in the labor movement who charge that the long contract has weakened DWU's clout with Cummins. Neihart, who now is in the real estate business, still wonders what will happen when the contract's two-tier wage system kicks in. So far, Cummins hasn't hired any workers at the $8 an hour rate that the contract allows for new employees. But eventually they'll be working alongside senior workers making more than twice as much. Some analysts suggest Cummins may have tied its own hands with a deal that has kept so many 40- and 50-year-old workers on its payroll. Company officials insist that their expanding international operations and growing business have offset the cost.

Meanwhile, Dowling says, "I'll never be sorry as long as we are working toward the same vision." Adds Neihart, "I still think we did the right thing as a union."

7

Grooming Global Managers

General Motors' latest auto plant, in Rosario, Argentina, is a template for companies entering the new world of global manufacturing. Plant manager Rudy Gundacker, who came from GM's efficient plant in Eisenach, Germany, welcomes a visitor with a tiny cup of strong Argentinean coffee and introduces his management team. Three of Gundacker's former staffers at Eisenach are on hand, as is one manager who had worked at Toyota's operations in Britain. A former manufacturing specialist at Nissan is also part of the group, as is a human resources specialist from Saturn's plant in Spring Hill, Tennessee. Rounding out the crew are staffers from GM's complex in San Jose de Campos, Brazil, which borrowed heavily from the Toyota Production System used in Japan and at GM's joint venture with Toyota in Fremont, California.

Around Gundacker, conversations are taking place in Spanish, Portuguese, and German, while Gundacker speaks to his visitor in English. But one common language is being spoken by all: the language of manufacturing. Discussing their goals for the plant, Gundacker and his team use terms like *kaizen, just-in-time inventories,* and *takt time.*

If Rosario was simply to have been another plant in GM's Latin American Operations, the easiest thing might have been to choose a plant manager from nearby Brazil. But GM wanted Rosario, and four other plants announced or under construction, to use the efficient manufacturing techniques implemented at Eisenach, which had marked GM's first push into central Europe after the fall of the Berlin Wall. The company is developing a single manufacturing process for the five new plants, with Rosario the first among them to use the new GM system. Says Gundacker, "You walk into any Toyota plant, and you know where you are. You walk into one of the (GM) plants and you will know, too." Thus GM turned to Gundacker, who is considered a maestro in the lean manufacturing world. "He is the best plant manager I have ever worked for," says Norman Bafunno, a former GM manufacturing manager who has since become one of three co-plant managers at Toyota's Evansville, Indiana, truck plant.

Gundacker is at the forefront of a new generation of global manufacturing managers. They are smashing the old stereotype that to be sent overseas and away from home plants was punishment. Today at Vanguard companies, international management experience is a prerequisite to climbing the corporate ladder. And being asked to manage a facility like Rosario is a sure sign of success. "If you're going to be the Vice President of Manufacturing in the future, you'd better have experience overseas," says Rich Freeland, manager of Cummins Engine's Columbus, Indiana, plant. Adds Chrysler CEO Robert Eaton, "I am a real strong believer in international experience. It makes you much stronger. I don't think you can ever understand a market without spending time there."

To join Dana's elite world operating committee, made up of its top 30 executives, a manager must have experience in three of six areas: manufacturing, finance, human resources, engineering, quality, sales, and marketing, plus at least one international assignment. Says Dana CEO Woody Morcott: "You want senior management that can think in another culture, that doesn't think like middle Indiana, that thinks like a different culture. And you can't get that without living there. You learn the culture as you learn the language. Otherwise I think it's sort of superficial—it's, 'which are the best restaurants in Geneva' instead of, "what do people in Geneva think about politics or whatever they talk about.' "

A 1996 study by consultants A. T. Kearney concluded that the days of the successful executive, manufacturing or otherwise, spending his or her career at corporate headquarters are fast disappearing. "The global leader of the next century will be more mobile and more culturally diverse, speak multiple languages and possess professional experience in a variety of environments," the study reports. As companies increasingly organize themselves along global business unit lines rather than geography, assignments in another part of the world are simply to be expected. Yet finding the right managers with the ability to handle life somewhere other than home is difficult even for Vanguard companies. Living on a vast continent whose shores are swept by two immense oceans, Americans are notorious for their reluctance even to vacation outside the United States, a trait that Dana Europe President Gus Franklin admits is a disadvantage for U.S. companies in the global race for business opportunities. "The average American wants to work 40 hours a week and wants to be home on the weekend. They're not great adventurers like the British or the Dutch. Even though we were founded by immigrants, we don't want to reimmigrate," he says.

Adds GM's Eric Stephens, "We don't have as much cultural sensitivity coming out of North America, and that's something you have to get under your belt from day one."

Yet despite the perception that U.S. companies have the hardest time finding global managers, consultants are finding it can be every bit as difficult for European and Asian companies to groom managers who can adapt to conditions elsewhere. "We have trouble with people in France and Germany just leaving their home town. It's not uniquely American," says A. T. Kearney Principal Alan Hammersmith.

All of the Vanguard companies have well-stated criteria for developing their global managers. Among the most important considerations:

- Multidisciplinary talent that will help a manager solve problems outside the specialty in which he or she is trained
- Flexibility on the part of the manager and his or her family
- Multicultural sensitivity that allows a manager to work comfortably with people who are not from his or her own background

- A collection of personal skills, such as expertise in a foreign language, comfort with computers, negotiating ability, and, simply, courage

But no global manager can expect to be a true success if his or her company has not defined its own goals. This is where a manufacturing process becomes especially critical. Chrysler's Eaton says the Chrysler Operating System (COS) ultimately will allow any manufacturing manager to walk into any Chrysler plant, whether it is in Sterling Heights, Michigan, or Cordoba, Argentina, and go to work. The Toyota Production System (TPS) allows Toyota managers from any part of the world to transfer smoothly to another location without having to learn "how we do things here." One extra advantage Toyota has is a team of Japanese coordinators on hand at all of its plants. It is this team's responsibility, in part, to make daily reports back to Japan on what is transpiring in the plants and to receive Toyota's latest updates on best practices. Cummins's performance charts make no allowances for a plant's location: All are measured on the same CPS performance criteria. All of Dana's business units worldwide are expected to embrace The Dana Way and to run themselves accordingly. If they don't, Morcott and other senior executives could show up on the scene unexpectedly to find out why.

Says A. T. Kearney's Hammersmith, "In a truly global organization, there are no longer home values. There are corporate values. It is an amalgamation of a company that does business in many markets."

Along with practical knowledge of the way a company is run, a global manager must utilize his or her own unique abilities outside the home office. Talent is particularly crucial because a global manager often serves as the face of the corporation to the local community. Dana Chief Financial Officer Jack Simpson, who ran Dana's Asian operations before ascending to the CFO's job, said he relished the opportunity to be Dana's "man in Hong Kong." His Asian assignment marked a return to familiar territory. He served in the U.S. Army during the Korean War and later spent extensive time in Asia in other Dana positions. As a regional president, Simpson says, "You're out in the field, you're a field commander. This is Norman Schwartzkopf, over there in the Persian Gulf, where he wanted to do what needed to be done." "I'm a field type guy. I really like that kind of action, dealing with the Chinese, dealing with the Koreans," he adds.

Where GM's high-potential employees (called "high pots") once competed for top posts in its New York Treasurer's Office, a proving ground for senior executives, they are now being encouraged to take positions outside of North America. For inspiration, they need only look to GM's governing President's Council, made up of its CEO and senior executives. Four of these top five executives, including CEO Jack Smith, all held international posts during their careers. Says GM International President Louis Hughes: "We want to send absolutely the best people. If we send some of our high potential managers, then other stars will want to go. We're looking for businessmen, we're looking for risk takers, entrepreneurial people, innovative people."

Yet what makes a manager successful in a home market might not translate into success elsewhere. Even if he or she is a proven performer, "it's very difficult to take a manager who has gone up the corporate ladder for years and then plunk them in Switzerland," says A. T. Kearney's Hammersmith. Yet that is exactly what companies have done for years, based on the long-held view that global assignments are cushy rewards for a job well done at home. "They'll say, 'I'm going to send Charlie over to Indonesia,' " not realizing that Charlie has never been to England, let alone a country where he can't figure out how to get from the airport to the hotel, Hammersmith says.

Vanguard companies have developed a number of ways to find out whether managers are suited to global assignments before they actually get on a plane. One is to put them on short-term projects that involve a global team of individuals from many different backgrounds. Sometimes they are located in the same place, such as the group that GM's Gundacker assembled in Rosario, other times they meet merely by telephone or video conference. This is happening increasingly at GM, Ford, and other auto companies who are developing vehicles that are sold in many countries, requiring expertise from engineers and marketing specialists in various regions.

On these global teams, conflicts quickly are rooted out. If a manager in Germany, brought up in an organization with an unquestioning respect for hierarchy, is offended by an American colleague's joking banter with the boss during a design meeting, it will quickly become clear that the German-born manager will need to readjust his expectations in order to prosper on a U.S. assignment. Similarly, an American engineer who wants to skip small talk and cut right to the chase once a meeting begins might have trouble getting to know colleagues in Japan, where small talk has been refined to an art form. Global teams help companies spot such red flags and solve them with training programs. By setting project deadlines, managers can insist that these global colleagues find a common ground in team sessions, or all participants will be viewed as having failed.

Once a manager demonstrates an ease in getting along with global colleagues on such teams, short-term international assignments of six months or less are often the next step, followed by longer placements of up to a year, and finally an extended assignment of three years or more. There's no set length for an ideal global assignment, says Dana's Franklin. "We don't have finite rotations. You can't plan these perfect increments. I'd say three years is enough to get some experience, but after five years you get sunk in. There's a need to keep fresh in your thinking."

On longer international assignments, there is no question that the cooperation of a candidate's family plays a key role. Moves can be particularly tough even within a candidate's home country: A recent survey by A. T. Kearney found 70 percent of managers were turning down moves within the United States for personal reasons. For two-career couples, transfers overseas can become a particular nightmare, because many countries, even in Europe, still routinely block a manager's spouse from taking a job that could otherwise be filled by a local resident. Franklin's wife, a lawyer, and Hughes's wife, a psychologist, each were initially barred from working in Switzerland despite their own long careers in the United States and their husbands' status as heads of their respective companies' European operations.

Some parents are hesitant to take infants and toddlers abroad for fear they cannot find proper medical care, especially in countries with emerging global markets. Flights from Moscow to Helsinki are regularly populated with expatriate parents and children who prefer Finland's hospitals and doctors to the uncertain quality of the medical attention they get in Russia. Similar concerns weigh upon a rising number of baby-boom-generation managers who face responsibility for aging parents. They don't feel comfortable dragging them across the world, nor do they want to be thousands of miles away in case of an emergency. Says GM's Stephens, "We can't afford to have situations where the breadwinner worries about the family problems."

These difficulties are prompting companies to reevaluate who should be sent overseas and the age at which they should be sent. Breaking with past practice, a number of companies are sending younger employees on international assignments because they are more accepting of uncertainty than are older managers. Some of these candidates are being recruited from colleges, universities, and competitors specifically to take global jobs.

"It's easier if you catch them early in their career, before there's a family situation," says Kearney's Hammersmith. "I would take the high potential people that you recruit and encourage them to go out on an international assignment."

This desire for "global-ready" employees is putting new pressure on graduate business schools, which are scrambling to add international focus to their previously finance-heavy curriculums. Yet sending employees out too early in their careers can be a risk. Negotiations with workers and with government officials are often delicate, and younger employees might lack the maturity that an older manager would bring to these situations. In countries such as Switzerland and Japan, where age is respected, sending a young manager to run an important venture can be seen as an insult. Simpson, who went to Asia for Dana at age 50, is glad that his international posting came relatively late in his career. "It wasn't a boondoggle for my wife and me. We hit the ground running. We were not there to live some elaborate life, all that ex-pat[riot] stuff that you hear about," Simpson says. "I was familiar with the region, I had a feel for how to work with the people, how to speak some of the language, how to get things done. Had I gone at 40, I don't know that I would have had the same appreciation that I had 10 years later."

Like Simpson, successful global managers need a set of survival skills to help them maneuver. One of those skills, says Stephens, is the willingness to break with local customs and get around barriers. When GM was building its plant in Eisenach, it wanted to implement just-in-time delivery of engines from its plant in Zaragosa, Spain, relying on a two-hour supply of inventory. But heavy truck traffic, combined with subpar eastern European roads, posed a major problem. Instead, the Eisenach management team, then headed by Stephen's predecessor, Tom LaSorda, decided to set up a dedicated rail line between the two plants. "The best professionals were telling us that it was absolutely impossible," Stephens says. GM now has been shipping engines on its rail line for eight years. It faces a similar problem in Brazil, site of a new factory nicknamed the Blue Macaw, set to open in 1999. Hoping to speed parts delivery from São Paulo, GM is investigating whether it can ship components by banana boats down the Brazilian coast.

"You have to be willing to question and change and challenge the status quo," says Stephens. Herb Bell, Chairman of Alexander Doll, calls it the "Noah principle." Says Bell, "At the end of the day, you've got to get the ark built."

Simpson recalls one visit to Korea where he was forced to rely on his wits. He arrived on a Monday hoping to wrap up a deal by the following Thursday, when he had booked a plane ticket back to Hong Kong. But his hosts, knowing when he was scheduled to leave, had filled his agenda with perfunctory meetings that Simpson knew would not lead to a contract. Suspecting that his counterparts were deliberately trying to sabotage the negotiations, Simpson went to an airline office and changed his ticket to an open departure. "When my Korean associates tried to lead me down their agenda, I stated very firmly that I had *my* agenda and I would not leave until I accomplished what I set out to accomplish," Simpson recalls. His hosts, startled, told him, "It is impossible for you to finish all of this and leave at 1 P.M. on Thursday." Simpson showed them his open ticket, and told them he was willing to stay a year if necessary.

Their reply was *chowayo, chal hapsida,* or "Let's do it in a nice way." The deal was done by 1 P.M. the following Thursday, as Simpson had planned. "It boiled down to endurance—what the Koreans call *innae,*" he smiles.

Along with nerve, Vanguard managers also have to show willingness to bend to local conditions when necessary. GM planned to use the same kind of worker training programs at Rosario that it uses at its Saturn plant. The programs are meant to foster teamwork between United Auto Workers members and GM managers. But during initial job screenings in Rosario, the GM officials discovered that their potential workforce in the heavily agrarian area had little understanding of what it would be like to do the repetitive work that takes place inside an assembly plant. Thus the company has already planned for additional training courses to make sure that workers will be able to handle an eight-hour day inside the plant without going crazy with boredom. And in a city where pony-drawn carts are still used by farmers to tote loads of corn to the marketplace, GM has found that many employees won't have their own cars, or even bicycles, to drive to work. So it has arranged for buses to transport workers to and from the plant each day.

"The challenge is taking Eisenach as a base and improving on it. You don't want to just copy what you did there," plant manager Gundacker explains. Adds Stephens, "I've learned so much from the people who've worked for me. If you don't learn to listen to your people in an international environment, it doesn't matter what your system is, you won't have any success in implementing it."

Yet just as companies' are finding that the need for managers who are comfortable in a global environment is accelerating, executives are encountering a serious obstacle: They cannot find the right people to fill the jobs.

"This is where companies really hit the wall," Morcott says. "It takes good people to run these operations, and you cannot always find people who are willing to go."

In December 1996, Russian Prime Minister Viktor Chernomyrdin darted from a snowstorm into a warehouse to open Yelaz-GM, a $250 million joint venture to build Chevrolet Blazers in the former Soviet territory of Tatarstan. Parts come from GM's Brazilian operations and are assembled deep inside a half-completed factory that was first intended to be a tractor plant, and then a small car factory. The building sits in the middle of a dilapidated industrial park, part of 155 square miles of decaying buildings constantly whipped by infamous Tartar winds that are icy cold in winter, blistering hot in summer.

"This is a victory—I cannot call it anything else," Chernomyrdin declared to the plant workers, none of who would be able to afford the $25,000 to $30,000 U.S.

dollars that the Blazers cost.[1] GM considered the plant a victory as well. It was the first automaker to push into Tatarstan, an oil-rich republic in Central Asia. Yet it could not find anyone inside GM to run the plant. Tatarstan is hundreds of miles from Moscow and Istanbul. Schools are substandard. Modern housing consists of a few apartment blocks. There is but one decent hotel, little shopping, few restaurants, and the only Western culture is found in videos. Despite the strategic importance of the venture, the drawbacks of daily life proved a real stumbling block to convincing many of GM's most promising managers to take charge.

Even in conditions not nearly as bleak as those at Tatarstan, candidates are rejecting overseas jobs largely for one fundamental reason: the fear that once away from the home office, they will be forgotten. In early 1997, Kearney quizzed executives, managers, and division heads of more than 120 global companies. It found that only 68 percent of employees who had worked overseas felt they had successfully transferred back home from international assignments. Many companies routinely brought employees back simply because their international stints were up, usually after three to four years. Among these employees, the average time waiting for a new assignment was six months.[2]

Fear of being forgotten is such an old cliché that many executives refuse to believe it is still true. "I'm sure that was true 10 years ago, but it can't be true now," says Cummins Chief Executive James Henderson. Perhaps it isn't at Cummins, where great emphasis is placed on international experience. But, says Kearney's Hammersmith, the fear is especially real at companies that are based far away from major metropolitan areas where top executives have not spent time abroad. "If you have a company in New York City, chances are you can get somebody to go overseas. But in Harrisburg, Pennsylvania, it's very hard," says Hammersmith.

As with embracing a global vision, convincing excellent managers to take international assignments requires direction from the top. Each year, Dana transfers a total of 50 managers from its corporate offices to international postings and from international postings back to Toledo, Ohio, and other divisional headquarters. Dana finds these candidates through a well thought out succession program. For each of its top 110 jobs, there is a waiting list at least three people long. The list actually has fewer than 330 names, since a promising person is generally in the queue for several different jobs.

Candidates at Dana are eager to take international jobs for two key reasons: First, Dana requires international experience for any executive to join its uppermost ranks. Second, Dana's promote-from-within policy ensures that its own managers are offered the most sought-after jobs.

The frequent reassignments are ideal preparation for the challenges of global business, says Dana Europe President Gus Franklin. A 23-year Dana veteran, Franklin has run a series of manufacturing operations and served as a "product parent" for the Spicer Division before landing the European job.

"The way you get prepared to handle business in a global company is to be able to handle change, and you're taught that," Franklin explains. "At most companies, you tend to go up a funnel—either funnel up a specialty, or spend all your time in accounting or marketing or one portion of manufacturing. You tend to spend 10 or 20 years in that specialty area and you only know that business. If you woke up one day after being a manufacturing guy for 20 years and you're sent to Bombay, you wouldn't know what to do."

Dana's promote-from-within system engenders its own internal network among its managers, Franklin says. So does its two-dimensional matrix, with product parents crossing regional operations. People around the world have numerous contacts throughout the company, either friends and associates culled along the way; or contacts in their own region or product category. A manager who accomplishes something in one part of the world will be quickly rewarded by at least two people—his or her regional president and his or her product parent. And Dana's atmosphere of constant communication, one of the tenets of the Dana Style, further fosters the attractiveness of international jobs. Says Franklin: "You don't have that 'not invented here' syndrome. You have a culture of total participation."

Franklin admits that sometimes he welcomes the idea of a transfer back to the United States. Both his children live in California, nine time zones away from Dana's Swiss headquarters outside Lucerne. "I have to make an appointment to talk to my kids," he smiles. But under Franklin, Dana Europe's revenues have shot from $490 million in 1992 to $1.3 billion in 1997. "Professionally, I think the opportunities and the action are outside the United States. That's fast growth anyway you cut it and that's fun."

The parochial approach that Dana has taken might not be possible at other companies, especially those whose ranks constantly turn over. Employee loyalty is a huge concern for many companies, which are growing weary of training managers only to see them stolen by competing firms for more money or better benefits. How can they make international jobs attractive to managers who fear being forgotten? Fundamentally, it comes down to changing companies' attitudes toward managers, says Anand Sharma, CEO of TBM Consulting Group.

"We talk about capital investment versus personnel expense," Sharma says. "The only appreciating asset that a company has is people. It'll be great to see corporate reports saying that we have invested this much in our people, instead of putting them on the expense side of the balance sheet."

Adds Lantech President Pat Lancaster, "You have to remember that these employees are our consumers. These are the people who will only stand in line at McDonald's for 16 seconds before they walk away. These are the people who are angry if they pull the computer out of the box and it runs into glitches as soon as they turn it on."

Remembering employees while they are on international assignments is also a key factor. One way to do this is through formal mentor programs that link a middle-level manager to a senior executive who is responsible for monitoring the manager's progress overseas. The senior executive makes sure that the international manager's interests are protected. The executive's bonus is decided, in part, on how well he or she looks after the overseas manager, and how well that manager performs once he or she returns to headquarters.

"I would call it a mentoring program with teeth," Hammersmith says. Such programs reflect a company's dedication to nurturing and developing its valuable managers, who can easily feel disheartened and isolated on overseas assignments regardless of access to video conferencing and e-mail. "It's tough enough in a single cultural environment. In a multicultural environment it's even tougher," Hammersmith says. But the challenge is not insurmountable if a company has identified and embraced what it means to be global rather than just an international player.

The enthusiasm of a company's top managers can also play a big role in retaining employees. GM's Hughes had to be convinced by his mentor, Jack Smith, to leave the New York Treasury Office and work for Smith when Smith was running GM Canada, and to subsequently leave Canada to work at Opel in Germany when Smith was named head of GM's European operations. But once in Europe, Hughes attacked his new assignment with glee. He began by taking a German immersion course so that he could give his first address to Opel employees in their native tongue. Hughes's colleague Mark Hogan, now in charge of GM's small car operations, took similar lessons in Portuguese when he was named head of GM do Brasil, as did his successor, Frederick "Fritz" Henderson, who took charge in Brazil in 1997.

Hughes and Hogan's emphasis on learning a second language has become so well-known inside the company that a staffer once phoned his boss and said, "I want an overseas assignment. Which language do I need to speak?" Now that he is running all of GM's international operations, Hughes says "I'd like to know Spanish, I'd like to know French, I'd like to know Chinese, and I'd like to know Japanese. Those are four languages that I'd like to be able to be fluent in. I know a bit of French, Spanish I can read, Japanese and Chinese . . ." he holds up his empty palms and smiles.

Adds Stephens, "You don't have to perfect, but you have to be part of the work environment. Without language skills, the impact is less."

At Dana, a second language is required for any manager sent to a non-English-speaking country for an assignment of two years or more. "If you go two years living in another country, you're expected to learn the language of the people," CEO Morcott says.

Europeans, exposed to many different languages by proximity, often smile at Americans' feeling of accomplishment at mastering another tongue. But even Europeans can run into confusion. One morning in August 1997, Renault executive Carlos Ghosn, who travels often, woke up uncertain of where he was. He could tell by the sterile surroundings of his darkened hotel room that he was not at home, outside Paris. But where was he—and more important, what language would he need to use? Was he in São Paulo, which meant he should begin thinking in Portuguese? In Frankfurt, which would require German? In Turin, necessitating Italian? Unable to find a clock, not even sure in which time zone he had awakened, Ghosn stumbled out of bed to peek through the curtains.

Below him in the distance lay Lake Michigan, glimmering in the August sunlight. Ghosn then realized he was in Traverse City, Michigan, where he was scheduled to give a speech in English that morning to a University of Michigan seminar on the challenges of globalization. He sighed in relief. Using English was no problem for the Lebanese-born Ghosn; until just a few months before, he had done business daily in English in his previous job as President of tire maker Michelin's North American operations, located outside Spartanburg, South Carolina.

Says Dana CFO Simpson, who speaks Korean and Mandarin Chinese, "It's very important that you be multilingual. However, you can't learn 10 different languages—you could but that would be all that you will be doing. You have business to conduct." To combat that weakness, Simpson made sure he was always accompanied by a staffer who spoke the local language. Smiles Simpson, "I never went unarmed."

One byproduct of companies' global push may be that Americans who never learned a foreign language may now feel they don't have to bother. Around the globe, English is quickly becoming a linguistic common denominator. In a café in Zurich, four managers— one Swiss, one Lebanese, one New Zealander, and one American—happily talked in English, their conversation punctuated by words in German and French that the quartet all understood. In GM's engineering labs in São Paulo, Brazil; Russelsheim, Germany, and Warren, Michigan, development work takes place in English. During his tenure as head of ABB, Percy Barnevik declared English the Swiss company's official language. Barnevik continues to uses English in his new position at Investor's new offices in London. CNN and Britain's SkyTV beam their English newscasts around the world, exposing millions of business travelers a day to the language. In Japan, numerous television ads featuring Hollywood stars are broadcast only in English. The wide use of the language seems to have removed a stumbling block that kept many Americans from even considering global assignments.

There is one tactic that Vanguard companies are using to overcome both language barriers and reluctance issues while building a corps of managers with global skills: They are handing over responsibility for key ventures to local managers. These individuals are hired with the promise that if they are interested, they will join the pool of managers vying for global jobs. Vanguard companies are finding that their global expansion has tapped into a new pool of talent that would have been outside their sphere of awareness had they remained in their home markets. At Dana Europe, just five of 7,500 employees come from Dana's home offices in Toledo, Ohio. The company's operations in India, with $50 million in revenue, have just three foreign-born managers, one American, one Canadian, and one Swiss. Says Franklin, "I can't see that you would manage 300 people going over and 300 people going back. You're going to have a lot of confusion. We have never found that we can run a local business better than local people. We're not local." He notes Dana is the largest automotive parts manufacturer in Venezuela, Brazil, and Argentina, and all of those factories are run by local managers, with only five American managers in total among the three.

"That's how it's going to continue to evolve. That's the way our business is going," says Cummins's Patel, whose fellow managers include Brazilian Roberto Cordaro, Group Vice President of Marketing. At Cummins's dozen facilities in China Cummins has individuals from Singapore, India, and Yorkshire working with local Chinese officials. "We don't have 20 Americans, we have 20 expatriates. We have a terrific core, we have assets, we have great partners," Patel says.

Dana CEO Morcott says the increasing diversity in companies must extend to boardrooms as well. Twenty-five percent of Dana's directors hold non-U.S. passports. "I don't think you're global if you don't have someone in your face who is not born somewhere else," Morcott says. He says U.S. companies are uniquely positioned to take advantage of foreign viewpoints, because of the nation's heritage as a melting pot and companies' willingness to hire non-U.S. citizens for senior management positions.

As examples, Morcott points to the Big Three U.S. automakers. At Chrysler, Vice Chairman Robert Lutz is Swiss, Engineering Chief François Castaing is French, and Advanced Manufacturing Chief Frank Ewasyshyn is Canadian. GM recently added Swede Barnevik to its board, while the head of the company's worldwide product development, Peter Hanenberger, is German, and Vice President of Corporate Communications John Onoda is Japanese-American. The top two executives at Ford, CEO Alexander Trotman and President Jacques Nasser, are Scottish and Australian, respectively, and Ford recently lured the former chief designer at Audi and Volkswagen, J. Mays, as the company's new head of worldwide design. Though an American, Mays spent much of his career working in Europe.

"That doesn't exist in Japan. It just doesn't happen. You don't have any non-Japanese in senior management," Morcott says.

Toyota's Okuda, whose management and board are, indeed, solidly Japanese, says he would like that to change. But he tends to waffle on the touchy issue. Okuda says language difficulties would make it hard for non-Japanese directors to fully participate in company affairs, even though Toyota's top management and directors, to a man (literally), speak English, and translators are readily available at all Toyota events. Asked if a non-Japanese board member will be named while he is president, Okuda shakes his head almost wistfully. "No, I do not think that will be the case," he replies.

Says author Womack, "There is a failing to the Japanese side that they feel a commitment to capital investment and human investment in their home markets. They haven't moved as quickly as they should have."

The willingness of management to welcome individuals from other cultures is a key advantage that U.S. companies have over their global competitors, says Dana's Simpson. During the 1980s, 90 percent of emigrants from the world's developing countries headed to the United States. By early in the twenty-first century, more residents of California may speak Spanish as their first language than English. In the United States, most business school graduates have headed off to their first corporate assignments by age 26; in Europe, where the equivalent of a bachelor's degree typically requires up to seven years of schooling, many students stay on to earn doctorates, meaning they are not entering entry level management jobs until age 30 or later. Simpson strongly disagrees with former GM and VW executive Jose Ignacio Lopez de Arriortua, who suggested that European managers may be best trained to deal with cultural diversity because of their frequent exposure to other languages, currency, and national characteristics within continental boundaries. Says Simpson, "If that's true, then why is America the number one country in the world in terms of productivity and globalization? We're good at what we do. We just don't give ourselves enough credit."

8

Beyond the Flavor of the Month

Some CEOs spend their summer holidays in the Hamptons. Others relax on Nantucket or take jaunts to the Tuscan hills. But in the summer of 1997, Cummins's Jim Henderson found himself in far-off Uzbekistan, on the shores of the Aral Sea. It was the first time he had been anywhere near "one of the Stans," as he puts it, that once were part of the Soviet Union and have since become autonomous nations.

Henderson's trip to Uzbekistan, which is wedged between Kazakhstan to the north and Turkmenistan and Afghanistan to the south, came at the invitation of Case Corporation's equally global-minded CEO, Jean Pierre Rosso. Case, which includes agriculture and construction equipment makers J. I. Case and International Harvester, landed an $80 million order from the Uzbeki government in May 1997 for 400 tractors, 200 combines, and 400 model plows, many of which use Cummins engines. As part of the deal, Case agreed to train local technicians to service the equipment. Rosso invited Henderson to Uzbekistan to investigate whether Cummins wanted to make its own investment in the region as well.

Other CEOs might delegate such a job to a local manager or the director of a business unit. But Henderson decided it was worth making the trip across 10 time zones himself. "There is no substitute for going there and seeing the culture. There has to be part of a mindset that says, 'yes, this is it!' " Henderson says, snapping his fingers. Even if Case hadn't suggested the trip, Henderson might have ended up in Uzbekistan at some point on his own.

"We are always out there looking for opportunities," says Henderson, relaxing in the relative serenity of his Columbus, Indiana, conference room. "Sometimes, our customers lead us into interesting places. This just happens to be one that a customer found before we did."

Henderson discovered Uzbekistan's culture to be somewhat similar to that of Turkey, a country he already knew because Cummins has a licensing deal in Izmir. And he was impressed by the knowledge of local managers, some of who had been schooled in the United States. "It's sort of the prototype of the ambitious country trying to move into world markets. It's a place that we are making sense of that we never would have before considered going," Henderson says.

CEOs who have never worried about shining their own shoes or filling their own gas tanks are now spending their time, like Henderson, in parts of the world they have never heard of. The rush is on to find the next hot global market, snag the next lucrative joint venture, and meet the next influential politician who will ease a company's path to a prosperous investment. And little wonder. Manufacturers invested more than $100 billion in new ventures around the globe in 1997, according to the World Bank. The World Bank also estimates that more than 20 percent of the world's Gross Domestic Product (GDP) is produced by the parents and foreign affiliates of multinational companies. Twenty percent of the world's manufacturing output is produced just by global manufacturers' operations in countries outside their home markets. And one-third of all the world's trade is conducted just by these multinational companies.[1]

"We stand at a unique moment in history," says World Bank Chief Economist Joseph Stiglitz. "New technologies, combined with continued economic reform and investment in education, offer the chance for developing countries to accelerate the development process—in some cases, by generations—and join the global economy as vibrant players."

The leaders of these countries go through a certain thought process that leads them to the global marketplace, says Henderson. "There's a logic train here," Henderson continues. "They're saying, 'I'm in power, I've got these people, what am I going to do for them? How am I going to raise the standard of living?' How do you do it? Do you do it by closing your borders? No, you immediately find out that's inefficient. You've got to invite in the right partners and technicians."

The opportunities have created nothing less than a stampede to enter the world market—and as in a real stampede, some are being trampled by the momentum. From Asia to central Europe, the Middle East and Africa to Latin America, new ventures are popping up every day in every corner of the world. By 2020, the

World Bank estimates the world's developing countries could account for 30 percent of the world's GDP, double their percentage in the 1990s. Already in 1997, developed, high-income countries such as the United States, Britain, and Japan, accounted for only 71 percent of the world's GDP, down from 84.2 percent in the early 1990s.

"This is a very favorable time in world markets. It is certainly the most favorable I've seen in my time in business," says Henderson.

But this is also the most treacherous time. Determining the appropriate global markets in which to compete is a nail-biting affair even for Vanguard companies, which are already equipped with the proper vision, resources, and tools. "It's not for the faint of heart," says Dana Chief Financial Officer Jack Simpson.

Selecting sites for global ventures requires a strategy all its own. One approach is to use the old journalism criteria for a properly written news story: answer the critical questions. When it comes to global manufacturing, however, the fundamental questions change from "Who, What, Where, When, and Why?" to "Why, Where, When, and How?"

WHY

The most-cited reason for justifying a global venture is competition. Everybody else in your industry is in China, ergo you must go to China as well. "You have to go because you can't give a competitor too much of a position in other parts of the world where the rapid market development is occurring. Otherwise, they will come back and eat your heart out on the capabilities that they've learned somewhere else. It's not something companies can avoid doing," says David Cole, Director of the Office for the Study of Automotive Transportation at the University of Michigan.

But woe to the company that goes international solely for that reason. Vanguard companies say there are just two basic reasons for launching a manufacturing venture outside a home market: the opportunity to serve customers in a developing market with your products, and the opportunity to make your own company stronger in the process.

"Number one, you don't do anything that's dumb and you don't do anything for cosmetic reasons of business. That's pretty high-priced PR work. You don't invest money and build factories for public relations," says Dana CEO Woody Morcott. "You do it because it makes a lot of sense, because your customers are there, because you want to grow. You may enter markets at a youthful stage of that market but you do it because you think it's going to grow and you're going to make a profit, not because it's the in thing to do and everybody else is doing it."

Says Lantech Chairman Pat Lancaster, "There is an excess of supply over demand. Just because we all rush to these markets doesn't mean that the people there are going to immediately run out and buy what we are trying to sell them."

Cummins Engine has no expectations of quick results for its global deals. It set up its joint ventures in China and India expecting that the two countries' truck markets will develop sometime in the next five to 10 years. "That's a bet that's going to pay off after the year 2000. We take a long look at the world and we say, 'where do we have to be if we are going to be a major player 10, 15 or 20 years from now?'" says Cummins President Tim Solso. Yet Cummins is already in a good position relative to its competition. Seventeen percent of its global revenue comes from Asia alone. By the next century, if Cummins has positioned itself correctly, half of all its revenue will come from outside the United States, with its Asian ventures playing a major role.

The attractiveness of new markets is one of two reasons University of Michigan Professor William Lovejoy suggests international investments are valid. The other is the opportunity for innovation. "If you are looking at Brazil as the Brazilian market, then your behaviors might be different than if you are looking at Brazil as a great place to manufacture," Lovejoy says.

Few financial executives can resist the cost benefits of doing business in Mexico or Vietnam, where workers earn about $47 a month, what European hourly workers earn in one hour. But manufacturing experts say this savings doesn't take into account transportation costs and delivery time, let alone market fluctuations, which can easily wipe out the advantage that low hourly wage rates can offer. It takes consumer products maker Black & Decker six weeks to ship appliances from a factory in China to the United States. By then, shifting consumer tastes can make the products obsolete.

"The idea of cheap labor is a real loser," says Jeff Trimmer, Chrysler Director of Operations and Strategy. Adds Shingijutsu President Chihiro Nakao, "I have to question why people are so tempted to go and establish plants in China, rather than the U.S. If this is the place of consumption, why not keep the production here?" He adds, "American people love to talk about cost. But top management in this country doesn't know what to see on the shop floor. In Japan, nobody talks about cost first. Cost is just a consequence of the effort of manufacturing. You don't hear about it on the shop floor—workers there just worry about quality."

WHERE

Choosing the correct market in which to build a manufacturing plant is sometimes akin to a crap shoot. Even when all the data a company collects points to success, external factors can play havoc with the best-laid plans. The emerging markets that are so attractive because of their potential are also going through growing pains that could last for several years, perhaps even another decade.

Consider what happened in Southeast Asia during the summer of 1997. In the early 1990s, investors flocked to countries like Thailand, Indonesia, Malaysia, and the Philippines, drawn by the countries' high savings rates, good education systems, open economies, and sound economic policies. Regional stock markets boomed, yielding investors profits of thousands of percents. From 1985 through 1995, the region, with a population of 1.7 billion, saw one of the most impressive economic ascents in history. The World Bank estimates per capita output rose by 7.2 percent per year in that time; per capita output in the United States, by contrast, barely rose 2 percent a year.[2]

But the "Asian Tiger," as the market was known, was suddenly defanged. On July 2, 1997, Thailand, once the region's boldest and most shining star, was forced by overhanging debt loads and its trade imbalance into humiliating devaluation of its currency, the *baht*. Worth roughly four cents on the dollar at the beginning of the summer, the *baht* ended the summer at about 2.8 cents, down 40 percent. Proud Thailand, whose citizens reveled in owning the latest $400 cellular phones and $2,000 Prada tote bags, was forced to go to the International Monetary Fund, Japan, and other lenders for a $17.2 billion rescue package. "Thailand is a shock," says Dana's Simpson. "That is a great example of a great institution that frankly failed."

The uproar caused shivers of horror at companies such as IBM, just putting the final touches on a $560 million hard disk-drive plant in Thailand scheduled to open in December 1997, and GM, which had selected Thailand as the site of one of its five new world plants. Its $750 million venture was set to open in 1999. Despite nervousness, however, the companies insisted they would stay the course: "In our long-term plans, we obviously expect there will be peaks and valley in the economies of regions and individual countries," GM spokesman Mike Meyerand said.[3]

But the crisis in Thailand was just a warm-up for what was to come. One by one, Asian markets and economies began to collapse like a long line of dominoes. Hong Kong's stock market crashed. South Korea fell apart, as its *wan* plunged to new lows. Indonesia was brought to its knees, requiring a bailout from the International Monetary Fund. Across the Pacific, Brazil's economy stalled, triggering two rounds of government emergency measures and plant closings. The biggest shock came in mighty Japan, long feared by its global competitors as an economic force. In just six months, the *yen* weakened by 20 percent against the dollar. A Toyota Camry that cost the equivalent of $19,000 to build in the summer of 1997 could be produced for just $17,000 by the following winter. Japanese leaders implemented a tax reform package, but not before banks and brokerage houses closed, prompting customers to bang on doors demanding that their funds be returned, and sparking tears from previously stone-faced chief executives.

No one could have predicted the extent of the Asian economic crisis. But Dana's Simpson spotted warning signs months before that trouble was brewing. The signals were contained in data that Dana keeps on every country in every region in which it does business. Flipping open a binder kept handy on his office conference table, Simpson walks a visitor through the criteria that Dana uses to decide where it should invest and how to gauge whether those investments are safe, including:

- Current account balances, which can show if a country has been too ambitious in attracting investors whose operations are adding little to the local economy
- The inflation rate
- Currency exchange rate fluctuations—has a country's currency had wild swings, which would indicate traders are losing faith?
- Total external debt, measured as a percentage of GNP, and in comparison to total exports
- Total debt service (i.e., the amount of interest a country is paying on its debt)
- Foreign exchange reserves, expressed in total and as a percentage of imports
- Sovereign debt ratings: How do rating agencies view the country's future?

"Watching the directional movement of these vital signs of a particular country or countries within a region is an imperative for a global company," Simpson says. He displays single-page sheets for each region, listing the names of the countries down the left hand side and the measurements across the top. A glance at each page gives a regional manager or product parent the opportunity to weigh one country's performance in a region against another's. "What we're trying to do is balance our business around the world globally so that any one region doesn't pull us down," Simpson says. These measurements, plus its customers' requirements and its own assessment of business opportunities, help Dana decide where it needs to be.

Some major decisions are a given. Nearly every executive, analyst, and student of global manufacturing agrees that to be considered global, a company must plant its flag in each of the key regions of the world: Europe, Asia, North America, and South America. The winnowing down process to determine where in each of those regions a company will establish operations is where the real decisions lie. Says Simpson, "We have only made that commitment to those specific countries that we thought were strategic. There are 40-some odd countries in Asia. We're only in 10. Just as we are not in every country in South America, we're not in every country in Europe."

Within those four world regions, the major focus of manufacturers in the 1990s has been on what the World Bank calls the "Big Five" developing countries—Brazil, China, India, Indonesia, and Russia. Today, they account for 50 percent of the world's labor force, but just 10 percent of its output and trade. By the year 2020, these five countries alone could account for almost 25 percent of the world's output and trade, or 50 percent more than the European Union countries enjoy today.

Of the five, the greatest focus has been on China for one basic reason: its size. China's population of 1.2 billion people dwarfs the population of India, the second most populous country with 950 million people, and is five times bigger than the population of the United States. If economic trends continue, China will have a GDP larger than the that of the United States within five years.[4] Even if its economic growth slows by half, economists predict China will surely surpass the

United States as the world's largest economy within 20 years.

The image that many Americans once had of China as a nation of automatons on bicycles, an image that first came to life during the Nixon Administration, is long gone. Now, the Pacific Coast corridor running from Hong Kong to the south and Beijing to the north shows signs of becoming as developed as any stretch of urban sprawl in the United States or South America. (Some analysts suggest, in fact, that China is almost two countries: the rural mass that exists in the vast bulk of the country, and this high-growth region on the coast.) Luxury hotels and office buildings gleam in coastal cities. The single universal symbol of economic prosperity—cellular phones—is seen everywhere. No longer is Beijing only a city of bicycle riders in Mao jackets. Western business-wear and T-shirts and jeans are the norm. Executives ride in sleek chauffeur-driven Mercedes, while streets are clogged with small Toyotas and boxy Volkswagens. VW, which has been building vehicles in China for 20 years, actually sells more cars per month there than it does in the United States.

A visitor might ask how people in China can afford these cars. After all, China's 1997 per capita income of $580 is minuscule compared to the United States's $27,000 per household. But there is a growing layer of affluence in China. And the market potential is staggering. Just assume that 10 percent of China's 1.2 billion people could achieve an average income of $6,000, the minimum auto companies say a country's consumers must earn in order for its citizens to afford small cars. (By comparison, $6,000 equals the average per capita income of Brazil and Argentina combined.) In China's case, 10 percent equals 120 million people. If only 10 percent of those people bought cars each year, that would still be a market of 12 million vehicles annually—the same as western Europe.

"Why be in China? I don't know that you *can't* be there," says Simpson. "The question is in what form? At what level? What's your patience tolerance? Are you going to endure some pain for awhile? Are you going to run for cover?" Ultimately, Simpson continues, "companies must decide, are you going to compete or retreat? I submit you go there to compete, not retreat."

But with China comes a particular headache: politics. The student uprising and subsequent crackdown in Tiananmen Square still haunts relations between China and other countries. The U.S. Congress regularly erupts in debate over renewing China's Most Favored Nation status, with some members reciting a litany of reported human rights abuses, including the use of child labor and sweatshops. Clinton Administration officials regularly lead trade missions to China, declaring relations have improved only to see some event occurring after the trips to threaten the newly restored relationship. All this is frustrating for executives eager to take advantage of China's vast economic opportunities. As Simpson emphasizes, "We deal in commerce, not in politics."

Cummins's Henderson argues that the presence of global corporations can be beneficial politically over time. "We firmly believe that when you're dealing with totalitarian governments, any kind of contact with the people in those governments to bring them into the world is helpful," he says. "There are going to be bumps along the way. Tiananmen Square was a big bump, but it was a reflection of a government that, over time, we want to continue to bring into the world of trade and not isolate." But Henderson acknowledges that political instability can engender business risk. "You've got to protect the interests of your shareholders. Should China somehow withdraw, or the rest of the world attempt to isolate them in a way that causes them to retaliate against us, we would have a loss of assets. At this point, our investment isn't so great that this would be a disaster for us, but over time our investment is growing. So, you have to watch that situation very closely."

Ranking just behind China in most companies' eyes is India, whose economy has grown an average 6 to 7 percent over the past few years. Since 1991, when India removed entry barriers and liberalized trade and foreign investment practices, exports have boomed. Like China, India is a paradox: In its sprawling population of 950 million people, there is a layer of wealth and a real middle class, accounting for as many as 250 million people. But the scourge of poverty still blemishes its major cities. The average per capita income is still a substandard $1,666. India has 17 official languages, 25 states, dozens of castes, and six major religions. Manufacturers also have found far more loyalty to locally produced products among Indians than many expected. This is reflected in the amount of foreign investment there. In 1996, only $2.6 billion was invested in manufacturing plants in India, while, by comparison, investment in China reached $42 billion. If it is to maintain its 6 to 7 percent a year growth pace, India will need to attract at least $10 billion a year in foreign money.

Luckily for India, there is no lack of companies willing to take a stab at investment in that country, at least as part of a joint venture. The prospects initially looked brighter for Brazil, which has overcome raging inflation, political instability, and soaring interest rates to become a beacon of opportunity for manufacturers, which are flooding into the country to build factories.

More than a dozen car plants are under construction or scheduled to open in Brazil in 1998, buoyed by predictions that auto sales in Brazil will double to about 4 million by early next century. Yet TBM Consulting Group Vice President Mark Oakeson fears an eventual shakeout: Most of the manufacturers, including GM, Ford, Fiat, Volkswagen, Mercedes, and Toyota, are building small cars aimed at the same buyers. "There just isn't enough demand for that many small cars," says Oakeson. Chrysler, by choosing to build Dakota pickups, may have spotted a market niche that others are ignoring, Oakeson says. In late 1997, Brazil caught "Asian flu" and suffered a market meltdown that was halted by quick government intervention. The episode forced automakers to scale back their optimistic predictions, and cut production about 25 percent for 1998. Even so, three new auto plants were announced in January, 1998 alone.

Unfortunately for Indonesia and Russia, the other two countries in the World Bank's "Big Five," there are still enough fears to keep many potential investors away. Indonesia's image was severely tarnished in fall 1997, when the country was covered by horrible smog from out-of-control forest fires, believed to have caused the deadly crash of an Airbus jetliner. Its swift economic downfall spurred a bailout by the IMF and sparked widespread political uncertainty. Stories of crime and crumbling economic conditions in Russia have kept many manufacturers away. Difficulties in reaching deals with government-controlled partners have frustrated others.

Yet all of these countries have one ultimate weapon: the thirst of numerous companies to get into the global game.

WHEN

On the surface, the question of when to go global seems to have only one answer.

"Now's the time. That's the way of the world," Simpson declares. Adds Dana CEO Morcott, "You have to be out there because you have global customers. You don't have local customers anymore. If they are local customers, they won't be for very long or they won't survive."

GM Europe executive Michael Nylin acknowledges that exploding growth is a "double-edged sword. Everyone sees the growth and everyone is building plants." Nylin notes that just to maintain its market share, GM will have to build additional plants besides the four it has under construction in Brazil, Thailand, China, and Poland. "These are just a down payment on what we will be able to do over the next 10 years."

Toyota, which will have not even started production at its Evansville, Indiana, truck plant by spring 1998, had, as of late 1997, already begun laying out ground behind the factory for an expansion. The company has selected a site in France for yet another plant, and is considering a possible fifth assembly plant in North America. In Brazil, site of a Corolla plant that is set to open in 1998, the head of Toyota's operations pleaded, "There is still time to [further] expand in Brazil. It is not too late."

Says Cummins's Henderson, "If we were limited to North America, our growth rate would not be as fast as it is on a global basis. There is a coming together around principles of economics for global companies. It is a wonderful time to go in lots of different directions."

Yet the chaos is causing one Vanguard company—

Chrysler—to pause to catch its breath and reassess exactly what it wants to do. CEO Bob Eaton has learned the hard way just what anxiousness can lead to. In 1994, Eaton traveled to China with then-Commerce Secretary Ron Brown and a DC-9 full of fellow CEOs. Several times during the trip, Chrysler was on the verge of signing a deal to produce minivans in China. It had already lined up a Taiwanese manager for the venture, and was ready to begin construction as soon as it got the government's okay. But Eaton had one condition the Chinese were not willing to meet: retaining the intellectual property rights to the minivan's tooling.

Chrysler had been burned in the late 1980s with its groundbreaking joint venture in China, Beijing Jeep, acquired when Chrysler purchased American Motors in 1987. Beijing Jeep is still in business, producing about 25,000 Jeeps a year at what Chrysler says is a profit. But even as Jeeps were rolling off the assembly line, Beijing Jeep managers spotted almost identical Jeeps under a Chinese nameplate scurrying through the city's streets. They discovered that the counterfeit Jeeps were being produced from nearly identical tooling to the machines Chrysler used in its own plant.

Seeking to avoid a second such episode, Eaton demanded assurances from the Chinese that the minivan tooling would remain Chrysler's own intellectual property. He could not win the promise and backed out of negotiations as a result. The deal went to Mercedes instead. (In 1997, Mercedes told the Chinese government it wanted out of the minivan venture; perhaps a sign that Eaton's decision to proceed with caution, and ultimately to back out, was a wise one. Regardless, China already had a willing taker for the project: GM.)

Chrysler was not alone in encountering problems in China. In 1997, both paper goods maker Kimberly-

Clark and auto parts producer Borg-Warner filed objections with the U.S. government after discovering that their Chinese partners had not honored the terms of joint venture agreements. Borg-Warner, in fact, found that electric power and water had never been arranged for its auto parts plant, while Kimberly-Clark maintained that its processes for making sanitary products had been stolen by a factory that had set up shop across the street. Chinese officials have denied the allegations. But Chrysler's experience has made Eaton perhaps the world's most patient CEO when it comes to launching global ventures.

"[Many companies believe] 'if we don't get in now, we won't be able to get in.' Well, we don't believe that," Eaton says. "As markets become more and more open around the world, there will be more opportunities to go in there. So we don't see any need to rush into any particular market. If we could have gotten into China in a bigger way than we are right now, we would have done it. We tried to do that and it didn't work out. So at this point in time, we aren't pursuing anything at all."

Chrysler's prudence has set back plans for a small car, dubbed CCV, that Chrysler hoped could eventually be built in China. The little auto, made from plastic panels derived from soda bottles, might eventually be suitable for other emerging markets down the road, Eaton says. Publicly signaling its change of plans, Chrysler has changed CCV's name from "China Concept Vehicle" to "Composite Concept Vehicle." Eaton sees no harm in biding his time, because that gives him a chance to wait out some turbulence he expects is on the horizon, especially in Asia.

"That whole area of the world looks a lot different today than it did one year ago, and one year ago, it looked a lot different than it did two years ago. I think anybody would tell you now that they expect considerably less growth in that area than they did one, two, and three years ago. Companies were betting there would be big growth in Thailand, and look what's happened there," Eaton says. "We all still believe it's going to be a growth market. But it's going to be different kind of growth. It's going to have a different slope," Eaton says. He is confident that there will still be room for Chrysler down the road.

In the meantime, Chrysler is concentrating on South America, where it opened a plant in Cordoba, Argentina, in 1997, and has two others under construction in Brazil, including one that is a joint venture with Germany's BMW. Whenever it wants to go to China, or Thailand, or any other market, its suppliers, such as Dana and Cummins, will already be there, ready to serve a key customer.

How

Foreign manufacturing ventures often require a road map, not only of the terrain being explored but of the business conditions that a company might encounter. Competition, local markets, economic factors, education levels, and political considerations all must be taken into account when deciding what kind of manufacturing venture is appropriate. At home, these types of questions are important, but certainly less so in light of the fact that most companies own their factories outright in their home markets. In a vast number of cases, the first manufacturing ventures Vanguard companies open in new markets are joint ventures.

Cummins has based much of its international expansion on joint ventures, which span the globe from England to Brazil, India to China. "I don't think any company, I don't care how big they are, can do it by themselves anymore," Cummins President Tim Solso says. Adds William Lovejoy, head of GM's Service Parts Operations, which produces replacement parts for GM cars and trucks, "You do things in joint ventures with your competitors that you would never try to do at home."

Cummins's method of investigating partners is unusual in the spreadsheet-focused 1990s, where potential profit margins often outweigh personal feelings of unease. As they consider possible joint ventures, Solso and Henderson say their first consideration is the personal feeling that they get from the other company's senior executive. This is in keeping with Cummins's often-stated corporate value "We do things the right way," but it can seem downright corny in the modern business world. Sitting in a Cummins conference room on a summer morning, the pair explains why executive empathy is so important.

"We're looking for people of like values. We believe the values of trust and integrity do cross cultural lines," Henderson says. You do some research, but fundamentally you have to decide is whether these are people you can work with." One method is the Cummins "dinner test." By hosting executives at backyard barbecues and holiday meals, Henderson and Solso say potential partners' true natures are often revealed in ways that wouldn't come across in business meetings. Says Solso, "Of the joint ventures that we have, I can't think of a senior guy in any of those companies that we don't like. We're friends. These are people you want to have in your homes. It's part of the fun."

A relationship between senior executives can help resolve differences when there are snags between indi-

viduals at lower levels of management. "The relationships have to be very strong at the working level and
they have to be strong at the top. They have to be strong
at both places," Henderson says. "It may be that there
are end users using our product somewhere that we
wouldn't be comfortable with. But we're talking about
partners."

A long-term attitude makes a difference, says Solso.
"If you look at this as a marriage, there will be good
times and bad times in that relationship. I can go to any
of our long-term relationships and point to dark days.
But the senior relationships are what allow you to do
the right thing and change what you need to change in
a joint venture." Asked if his instincts have ever been
wrong, the baby boom executive smiles. "Have we ever
been burned? There are times in an existing JV where
we fought about levels of investment, or levels of technology."

But those are issues that must be addressed as the
partnership discussions unfold, Henderson says. He
ticks off Cummins's criteria for joint deals. "For us, an
important partner is one that eases the entry (to a key
market). We're not in that situation in every case, but
that's ideal for us. The partner brings volume. We bring
comparative advantage to the partner. It's also important if the partner is strong, understands the local market and the culture, understands how business is done
in that venture," he says.

Adds Solso, "We prefer a 50–50 deal, although that's
not a hard and fast rule. But the mindset that we have
is that you have to think of what's best for the joint venture, not what's best for the parent company, even
though the parent company may try to influence that."

Typically, Henderson says, Cummins provides
money, training, and technology. And Cummins does

not follow many companies' practice of sending older technology and products to new markets in hopes of squeezing more profit out an investment that's already been amortized at home. Instead, Cummins and other Vanguard companies increasingly are sending new products to their emerging markets in order to meet the demands of newly savvy consumers. "We're willing to bring our best technology, our best products, and our best beliefs. There was an old way of doing things to which I think some people still cling, of sending your old technology, your old investment. It doesn't work," Henderson says.

Mercedes found that out in India in 1995, where the company owned a plant to produce its E-class sedan, aimed at India's expanding upper-middle class. Yet the E-class Mercedes chose to produce in India was not the streamlined car with distinctive round headlights that has been a hit in other world markets. India got the predecessor to that car, which is boxy, conservative, and less efficient. Consumers rejected the car in favor of up-to-date BMWs and Jaguars. Now, Mercedes's plant is operating at only 10 percent of its 20,000 car capacity. The company faces the prospect of either shipping expensive tooling to the factory and overhauling it, or continuing to build the old E-class and hoping that less savvy customers in Africa or Latin America might want to buy the car.

In hindsight, Mercedes's miscalculation was a surprising move for a company so willing to go out on a limb with its M-class in the United States. But author James Womack suggests Mercedes fell victim to the old assumption that foreign markets' value lies in lower labor rates. "When companies used to look at globalizing, they looked at the idea of lowering their labor cost. You would take low-technology, high-volume operations to a place like Thailand, and keep low-volume, high-content operations at your mother ship," he says. "That concept is totally obsolete now. What companies are striving for is to become 'trade neutral,'" where their local investments [around the world] are as great as their production at home."

Taking new technology to foreign markets can be a tremendous risk. Three months after it introduced its twisting Snake Light flashlight, which is made in China, Black & Decker saw virtually identical copies on hardware store shelves. Says Cummins's Henderson, "Well-meaning people say to us, 'Why are we taking our own technology?' We've got to have a mindset that says, 'We're going to obsolete our own technology, giving the customer the greatest value.' And therefore, we don't have to worry about that product coming back at it from the rest of the world."

Says Dana's Morcott, "The only way to penetrate the market is through product innovation. You've got to find ways to offer your customer improved features and improved durability at a lower price, and yet at the end of the day, you've got to stay in business from a profit standpoint. The only way you can do that is through new technology."

Dana Europe President Gus Franklin adds that no company can be successful in global ventures unless it is willing to outrun its competition. "We have to be ready to say, 'We will go as fast as it takes,'" Franklin says. That means being prepared to buy out joint venture partners as needed when economic or business conditions dictate.

The key to successful global ventures, says Franklin, is flexibility. "People are always talking about reengineering, restructuring. Well, you're always doing it. Once you accept that fact, you don't take it as a negative, you take it as a positive. You've got to be willing to change to go forward," he explains. For inspiration, Franklin cites the world's top golf professionals. "They are always fiddling with their game. You know, they say that Arnold Palmer has 5,000 clubs in his den. He's always trying to find a way to do it better than before. If you can imagine Arnold Palmer is always looking for a better way, then it must work for the rest of us."

9

Are We There Yet?

The swift charge of companies into both developed and emerging markets offers alluring growth to firms that have feared they would stagnate in their saturated home markets. Opportunities to manufacture at lower cost; free of restrictive work rules and uncooperative unions; and with no resistance to the latest technology is nirvana for managers who can't clear the hurdles of dealing with workers in their own backyards. The ability to show off a growth-dominated balance sheet to an impatient board of directors, skeptical shareholders, and demanding Wall Street analysts is enticing to any CEO.

Yet along with its potential benefits, global expansion also threatens to leave even the best firms drained of their resources, devoid of a solid strategy, and deserted by their finest people, some in search of better opportunities and others burned out by the global drive.

"There will be a lot of home runs, but also a lot of strikeouts," says Herb Brown, Chairman of Alexander Doll, who has chosen to overhaul his company's factory in Harlem rather than seek lower quality and less reliable sources of production outside the United States.

Vanguard companies, which are already excelling at manufacturing top-quality products outside their home borders, are aware of the pitfalls that lie ahead of them. They long ago removed the rose-colored glasses that many executives still don when gazing at the globe. Just as they have devoted countless hours to developing and implementing their globalization strategies, so, too, have Vanguard companies compiled a list of priorities that will govern their operations as they expand around the world.

BALANCE NEEDS OF CORE OPERATIONS WITH PUSH TO EXPAND ABROAD

It is utterly impossible for a company to fund a globalization drive from a position of weakness at home. Vanguard companies have learned that when danger signals sound, or when conditions dictate, they must address the fundamental issues facing their companies or else endanger the growth that would make them even stronger.

When 1997 began, Chrysler appeared to be in its best position ever in the U.S. car market. In 1996, it had captured 16.4 percent of car and truck sales, the most in its history, thanks to strong selling minivans, the Dodge Ram pickup, and its Jeeps. Yet in late spring, Chrysler began hitting potholes. Minivan sales softened significantly, forcing Chrysler to offer fatter rebates. Jeep sales began to lag in the face of Ford's newly introduced full-size Expedition sport utility. Even Chrysler's pickup truck sales, which had been so strong the year before, began to weaken. To top it off, Chrysler was hit by a month-long strike by workers at an engine plant in Detroit that cost it $750 million in lost production on one of its most popular vehicles.

All this came as CEO Robert Eaton had just snipped the ribbon opening Chrysler's new plant in Cordoba, Argentina, and as plans for its truck plant in Campo Largo, Brazil, were moving forward.

The company did not panic. Eaton and his management team acted swiftly to keep a lid on company costs while the automaker sorted out what had gone wrong. Wall Street analysts initially were told that over the next few years, Chrysler wanted to slice $1 billion of its annual $5 billion in capital spending, which pays for product development, manufacturing plants, and new equipment. But as the losses deepened and the truck market did not rebound, Eaton told his managers to turn up the heat. The cost-cutting goal became $1 billion for 1997 alone, and Eaton wanted to see the cost cuts continued in the following years. None of the moves affected Chrysler's international growth, and none of them delayed any of the vehicles that Chrysler planned to introduce over the next year, such as replacements for its midsize LH sedans. This was yet another example of how quickly the company was able to react when problems arose.

"Speed and flexibility are absolutely critical," says Lantech President Pat Lancaster. Adds Chihiro Nakao, President of Shin-Gijutsu Company, "You have to keep facing the challenge."

Part of facing that challenge is to keep investing in older factories, the so-called "brownfield" plants. Cummins, in Columbus, Indiana, has demonstrated a clear willingness to focus on its existing facilities at the same time it is expanding overseas. It used one of these facilities, the Columbus Mid-Range Engine Plant, as the incubator for its Cummins Production System. By reaching an 11-year contract with the Dieselworkers Union, Cummins expanded its commitment to its other operations in Indiana, particularly its main engine plant, where it will begin building the Signature 600 engine in 1998. Chrysler is currently in the midst of a series of investments in its older plants and existing plant cities, including Newark, Delaware; Detroit, Toledo, Ohio; and Kokomo, Indiana.

Chrysler and Cummins are willing to invest in these older plants in part because they are short on production capacity at a time when their operations in the U.S. market are growing. GM is in a different situation. It embarked on its global growth plan while it still faced cutback decisions in the United States and Europe, its most mature markets. That has let to some poignant situations. The demise of GM's aging Buick City complex in Flint, Michigan, is a case in point. Built in the 1920s, Buick City sprawls across 14 blocks in a deteriorating neighborhood on Flint's north side. The multilevel plant, obsolete by any modern standard, has been on its deathbed numerous times in the past. But it got a new lease on life in the late 1980s, when GM decided to embrace a team-based work system. The quality of Buicks built there improved dramatically, and even in 1997, Buick City ranked third on a list of GM's U.S. car plants in building cars with the fewest number of customer complaints. (Outranking Buick City were NUMMI, GM's joint venture with Toyota, and Saturn.

Both NUMMI and Saturn operate under special union contracts that eliminate many of the work rules and job classifications that stymie GM's efforts elsewhere.) Buick City's union members were particularly proud that the plant outscored two newer GM plants that built similar sized cars, one in Orion Township, Michigan, and the other in Detroit.

Yet, in 1996, GM canceled plans to build a new $250 million flexible body shop at Buick City that would have given the plant the ability to build more than one kind of vehicle, and said it had no new product planned for the plant after 1999. The move set off 18 months of efforts by community and union leaders to save the factory. Upon hearing rumors that GM was about to make a final announcement, Michigan Governor John Engler even met face-to-face with GM CEO Smith in November, 1997, to offer more than $250 million in tax incentives and other financing if GM would invest $1 billion to build a new vehicle in Buick City. But Smith turned him down. GM had too much car-building capacity to keep Buick City open. The automaker's deteriorating U.S. car and truck market share left it with little choice, he said. GM announced in late November that the plant, and a nearby V-8 engine factory, would close in 1999. And the shutdowns might not be GM's last. In the next decade, GM could build as many as 10 new assembly plants in markets outside North America. But in an echo of the drastic cutbacks that the automaker initiated at the start of the 1990s, analysts say GM may end up closing at least three of its home market facilities if the company cannot improve its dwindling sales. Says GM North American Operations President G. Richard Wagoner, "I can't make any promises to anyone."

Like GM, Vanguard companies know that in order to

face global competition, their operations will be in a constant state of flux. In 1997, Dana embarked on an extensive round of divestitures and acquisitions totaling more than $700 million, or nearly one-sixth of its annual revenues. Every month brought a new announcement of a business Dana was exiting or a company that it had acquired. The timing of the moves certainly was not ideal, given the company's quest to draw half of its revenues from outside the United States by the year 2000. Another company might have put the divestitures off until it had reached its goal, or simply bought the new companies and sorted out the collection later. But CFO Simpson says the moves were necessary to give Dana the clarity that it needed to focus on its core businesses. "What we're trying to do is balance our business around the world globally so that any one region doesn't pull us down," Simpson explains.

COURAGE TO WITHSTAND FADS AND STICK TO CORE VALUES

What will the global manufacturing world look like in 10 years? Will Vanguard companies have set up sparkling new satellites, be filled with the latest computerized automation and lowest-wage workers, be producing highly profitable products that are embraced by newly rich, consumption-hungry consumers?

Probably not. If anything, the world's best global companies will spend the next decade focusing on the basics of efficient manufacturing, finding the right mix between automation and labor, and carefully selecting products they think will sell to customers just enjoying their first taste of disposable income. Womack notes that Dana, despite its clear position as a Vanguard company, still lacks a manufacturing process. CEO Morcott says this is because Dana builds many types of products that can't be governed by one production system. He says Dana's internal measurements, such as The Dana Style and its Dana Quality Leadership Award, are workable substitutes for the statement of philosophy and process that an operating system would provide. It is a great source of pride at Dana that its leasing operations won the Malcolm Baldrige National Quality Award in 1996, even though the company did not take a top score on the DQLA rankings, which measure a range of elements, from productivity to quality and customer satisfaction.

GM, too, does not yet have a manufacturing system despite its expansion around the world. GM officials have adopted the motto "Run Common, Run Lean" and the company is striving to implement similar production methods in its factories through a common "bill of process," which sets out specific manufacturing methods that should be used in each of its plants. GM is trying to implement this bill of process while it is working on a formal manufacturing system in North America. In the five new plants it is building around the world, GM is moving a step further and is drafting a system that will be implemented as each plant opens. It has already begun that task with its Rosario, Argentina, plant, which opened in late 1997. When all five are open, early next decade, GM will then have a semblance of a manufacturing system that it can use as an example to its North American factories as what it is striving to accomplish. By then, all the North American plants should have implemented at least pieces of the bill of process, and GM hopes it will be only a short step to a manufacturing system from there. However, Cummins's Joseph Loughrey doubts this approach will work to GM's advantage. For one thing, the five plants are scattered geographically, making it time-consuming and expensive for people in GM's primary production centers to see what's going on. "That's too diffuse. I'd think you'd want to at least try to do something all at once," Loughrey says.

Lantech President Pat Lancaster agrees there's no substitute for seeing a process in action. But he says he is constantly surprised by the deluge of visitors to his tiny Louisville, Kentucky, factory. Lantech's efficiency in Louisville is highlighted in James Womack's 1996 book *Lean Thinking*. Lancaster has now had to limit tours of his facility to once a month to keep his 300-member workforce from being distracted. Once, 250 executives crowded into the small space where Lantech manufactures its shrink-wrap machines. Lancaster often wonders what visitors are trying to learn, since the lean manufacturing ideas that he has embraced have been in the public domain for a decade. He still shakes his head over the fact that none of his competitors have tried the same tactics to improve the efficiency of their plants. "They have not exactly knocked us over," Lancaster marvels.

He attributes the lack of interest in becoming more efficient to "an old boys club that's allowed them to get away with their old systems. The CEOs might want to try it, but the managers get it in their head that 'I'll do anything to avoid it.'"

Going global is a great excuse for a company to look past its fundamental problems because it's too busy trying to find new market opportunities to dwell on them. Yet in many cases pressing into global markets only unveils a company's core inefficiencies. Mistakes made in home markets are magnified once a company sets up a manufacturing operation elsewhere. Conversely, a well thought out, well-understood manufacturing process or operating system is an invaluable tool once a company decides to expand elsewhere. Obviously, a company can't expect to pick up everything that works in Omaha and drop it down in Argentina. In their book *Built to Last,* authors James Collins and Jerry Porras make a distinction between implementing a company's core values outside its home market and trying to use the same tactics and practices. "For example, Wal-Mart should export its core value that the customer is number one to all of its operations overseas, but should not necessarily export the Wal-Mart cheer," they write.

But, says Dana's Simpson, "Dana is Dana around the world. We can't be naive to think that our value system is the same around the world, but we believe in what this diamond [Dana logo] stands for."

Such focus is crucial as global manufacturers look toward the next decade. Turbulence is likely to be the rule in developed markets like Europe, where many companies are only now on the verge of the kind of streamlining and cutbacks that U.S. companies faced during the late 1980s and early 1990s. Europe has not yet gone through the massive waves of downsizing that afflicted U.S. companies—and, despite excess capacity in every corner of the continent's manufacturing operations, such cutbacks may never occur. Angry workers went wild in 1997 over plans by Renault, Ford, and Electrolux to close plants and trim jobs, launching massive demonstrations in the streets of England, France, and Belgium. When GM tried to conduct an evaluation of its main Opel factory in Russelsheim, Germany, in September, 1997, Opel's works council obtained a court injunction blocking a GM team from entering the company's own factory. The injunction coincided with a

painful round of negotiations on a new contract between Opel and its autoworkers union, and it reflected
the workers' fear of losing jobs as GM expands in other,
lower cost countries.

United Auto Workers President Steve Yokich, whose
union has lost nearly half its membership in the past 15
years, talks of joining forces with European, Asian, and
Latin American labor unions to keep U.S. companies
from fleeing their responsibilities to their workers. "It
matters where they're going, and where they put the
investment," Yokich says. "I think you take organized
labor around the world, and we've got to work together." In 1997, the UAW sent a delegation to Japan to
a meeting with union leaders there, breaking 13 years
of silence between the two labor movements that began
with Japanese automakers' expansion into the United
States "We're working closer together and they're
working with us," Yokich says.

But this solidarity may not be enough to withstand
the winds of economic change that lately have been affecting even those developing markets that have en-
joyed uninterrupted growth in recent years. The 1997
summer market meltdown in Asia may just be a pre-
view of what might be expected as markets in developing countries expand and contract. Few Vanguard
members expect the rapid pace of growth in regions
like Latin America and Asia to continue unabated. Yet
they also don't believe governments whose countries
have attracted new investment will allow economies
to get out of hand the way Brazil and Argentina did in
the early 1990s. Says Cummins's Henderson, "There is
a recognition throughout most of the world right now
that governments need to raise the standard of living
of their people. To do it, they need to provide jobs.
They need to attract foreign investment. To attract for-

eign investment, they have to run their economies reasonably well. The days of runaway inflation don't work."

SENSITIVITY TO MARKET CONDITIONS AND CUSTOMER NEEDS

Even when crises do arise, as they did in Thailand and Korea during 1997, Vanguard companies are determined to stay on course. The way they do so is by developing a fine-tuned sensitivity to all the factors that affect their global operations, particularly what customers might want. In fall 1997, Toyota surprised its competitors by announcing it would introduce three cars in India within two years. One of them would be a vehicle designed only for India. Toyota calls it a "family car" and it is able to hold up to 10 people. Described as a "slick-looking Jeep," it is similar to a vehicle called Venture that is sold in South Africa, and it is likely to compete with the Sumo DX that is made in India by Tata Engineering and Locomotive.

Toyota's move was a sharp departure from other companies' decision to first broach India with small cars, which they had assumed would be all consumers could afford. Certainly Toyota could have taken the easy way out by retooling a version of its Corolla for India. But Toyota studied the Indian market and found no one was paying attention to the multipurpose vehicle market. It expects this family car to appeal to large families, small businesses, and local governments. By the year 2000, India's car market could top 1 million units, and Toyota could have the large vehicle segment all to itself instead of competing with a dozen others for the small car market.

It was the same such reasoning that led Chrysler to build Dakota in Brazil, Cummins to produce its efficient Signature 600 diesel engine for North America, and Honda to take another crack at Japan's midsize car market with an all-new Accord that was designed primarily for the United States but includes the features that Japanese consumers have been demanding. None of these companies would be taking these steps if they had not first taken the pulse of the market. They evaluated their competition and decided to go in a slightly different direction. Often this requires an organization listening to local voices, something that is hard for a manufacturer to do without diversity in its ranks.

Another equally crucial talent is to stay realistic in light of predictions of massive change in consumers' lifestyles. Consider for a moment what life was like in the United States in the mid-1960s. People lived in houses; went to work in offices by train, bus, or car; talked to friends on the phone; watched television in the evening; went to movies on the weekends, followed by a meal at a restaurant; and took vacations to Europe and Florida on jet planes. In the 1990s, people still do all those things. What has changed are the details. Today, both a husband and wife in a household may earn an income, with one or both of them having a job based right in their house. Today they and their children might spend some evening time surfing the World Wide Web for entertainment. The family car might be a minivan or a sport utility or even a pickup. But the fundamentals remain the same. The typical American today is no closer to living the life of the Jetsons than someone in the 1960s, when the futuristic cartoon first hit the airwaves.

CREATIVITY: FINDING WAYS TO DO MORE WITH CORE BUSINESSES AND PRODUCTS

It is the details that matter most to Vanguard companies, which have already mastered the fundamentals of global manufacturing. The days when manufacturers could simply dump old tooling and outmoded products on foreign consumers are over, but globalization still offers them the opportunity to use the skills and products that made them a success at home in new markets.

"You can't say that there is growth in the U.S. per se [for automotive components]," says Dana Europe President Gus Franklin, referring to the fact that sales have stalled the past four years at about 15 million cars and trucks. "But there are so many growth opportunities in the world that we are in a growth company," Franklin adds. GM estimates auto sales worldwide could climb by another 10 million units, to 40 million units a year by the year 2010. With Dana now situated in the four key corners of the world's auto market, the company's potential for new business is enormous, even if it simply grows proportionately with its current customer base. Says Franklin, "That's what makes it exciting."

No one in the United States would think of Cummins Engine as a growth company either, with its core businesses in power generation equipment, industrial power, diesel engines, and heavy-duty trucks. But CEO James Henderson argues that Cummins couldn't be more perfectly situated to serve developing countries. "There's a progression. Power generation is the first thing that they need. They need power to move on their rivers," he explains. "Then they start building their roads, then they start building their infrastructure, then pretty soon the highways are in place. Then you get buses and highway trucks, then personal use vehicles." Cummins has been surprised at just how strong the world's truck markets have the potential of becoming. Says Henderson, "We once thought trucks were not a growth industry. In fact, trucks are the most efficient way to implement just-in-time inventory. Rail just cannot compete." So as other manufacturers open their plants, they are even more reliant on vehicles that use Cummins's engines.

Vanguard companies also are learning to leverage their creativity to make the most of their global investments. Toyota's Georgetown, Kentucky, plant would be a success by any measurement simply because of the popularity of the Toyota Camry sedans built there. In 1997, Camry was the best-selling car in the United States for the first time, surpassing Ford Taurus, the leader for the previous five years, and Honda Accord, which held the crown from 1989 to 1992. If Toyota wanted to ensure dominance of the midsize car market, it could have dedicated both Georgetown plants to Camry. That would have guaranteed it a supply of more than 520,000 Camrys a year, well beyond what Honda could build in Marysville, Ohio. But that is more than Toyota could expect to sell in the U.S. market, where it took the crown in 1997 with sales of about 399,000 Camrys. And Toyota saw ways to create new vehicles by using the Camry chassis as a base. In 1995, it stretched the Camry platform to create the full-sized Avalon, which sold for about $30,000, as compared to Camry's top price of about $25,000. In 1997, Toyota added the Sienna minivan, derived from Camry and selling for about the same price. In 1998, Toyota is expected to introduce the Solara coupe, also drawn from the Camry platform, which will be produced at its plant in Cambridge, Ontario.

Once Solara is in dealerships, Toyota has the potential to get 570,000 vehicles in North America off a single car platform—360,000 Camrys; 80,000 Avalons; 80,000 Siennas; and 50,000 Solaras. In Japan, where it has a broad lineup, Toyota would not have to leverage one platform to get so much product. But in North America, it has the opportunity to stretch its engineers' skills and its production resources to see what it can do. The Camry-platform cars are in addition to whatever Toyota does with its T-150 pickup truck, set to go into production in 1998 in Evansville, Indiana. The possibilities include a Toyota version of the Lexus RX 300 sport utility, the first entry in the U.S. market of a carlike SUV, or "hybrid." Toyota executives say they're concerned that the market for big sport utilities, like Ford Expedition and Chevrolet Suburban, could diminish in the next decade because of concerns over the vehicles' fuel economy and pollution. A hybrid would be more environmentally correct—and Toyota would still be well ahead of its U.S. competition. GM wants to offer hybrids in the next decade but hasn't begun development yet. If Evansville is expanded, Toyota will be well on its way to selling 1.5 million vehicles in the United States, a goal that seemed out of reach only a decade earlier when Japanese automakers' hands were tied by a strong yen and political pressure. Even if the yen were to drop below the 100 yen to $1 ratio, as it did in the early 1990s, Toyota eventually will have more than two-thirds of its U.S. sales in locally developed and manufactured products. Its Japanese base, though still vitally important for engineering resources, thus becomes less important.

Getting close to the customer is one goal of every Vanguard company as it proceeds on its global manufacturing path. It is a reason why Cummins, in recent years, has focused on developing a technical process, akin to its Cummins Production System, that guides engineers working in Cummins ventures around the world. By controlling product development, Henderson argues, Cummins can mitigate the risk it faces in emerging markets where its technology can easily be lifted by its competitors.

"One reason you have the technical operations in these diverse markets is that often, getting the specifications right is a technical job," Henderson says. "Being able to translate those to the customers' needs is an advantage of having skills close to the ground. You have to think beyond geographical boundaries. There's real value in them understanding the local values and the local needs of the customers on an ongoing basis." Adds Dana's Simpson, "We need to control our technology and in a place like India or China you can't always be sure about that."

GOING BEYOND GLOBAL

Is there anything global manufacturers can be sure of in the decade to come? Will this race to open plants turn out to have been simply a fad of the 1990s, only to vanish in the next century as companies realize they have stretched themselves too thin? Will companies find that the downsizing of the 1980s and 1990s backfires on them in a new generation of managers able to call the shots on where they want to go, what they want to be paid, and how they want to operate?

If anything threatens to stymie the push outside home country borders, it is the very fickleness of consumers. This can only increase as telecommunication, the wonder tool of the 1990s, backfires on the markets that it helped to fuel. As Mercedes found in India, there was no need to accept an old E-class sedan when ads for the latest model could be seen on CNN. As companies doing business in Brazil are likely to learn, once consumers' incomes begin to rise there will be a myriad of ways for them to spend that money, meaning no manufacturer can count on a lock on any portion of market share without putting the same effort into winning or retaining customers in Brazil that they do in Europe or the United States. As companies like GE have discovered in central Europe, just because they took a chance sooner on an emerging market such as Hungary doesn't mean that they are guaranteed that market's loyalty forever. In 1997, a Hollywood studio chief remarked that it would be safe to launch the heavily over-budget movie *Titanic* at the Tokyo Film Festival two months before its U.S. debut because "nobody hears about what happens there anyway." Nobody, that is, except the millions of viewers who turn to CNN each afternoon for its entertainment report, and the young internet fanatics who surf home pages looking for the latest industry gossip. (Luckily for the studio, the movie was a huge hit.)

Such instantaneous transmission of the world's trends leads Dana's Simpson to predict the next decade is likely to lead to a "universal market," where trade restrictions, local preferences, and cultural differences are offset by common aspirations. "I mean universal in terms of living together in one global community," Simpson says. "The world is going to get smaller and we are all going to become universal players. Everybody wants to trade with each other. We all dress alike, we all want to feed our children."

Corporations' push in recent years into new markets has made the trend irreversible. "Watch out. You have cell phones, laptops and the Internet in Africa and Korea and Vietnam. I never thought I'd talk to another Vietnamese in my life and here I am doing business with them," Simpson says.

Yet, universality does not make the task of operating global companies any easier. If anything, it simply makes the task of global manufacturing tougher because the competition can keep a close watch on where a company is headed, what terms it has commanded and what features its products possess. It adds up to enormous pressure that can make even Vanguard companies weary. Says Simpson, "We get anxious at times. Every company gets anxious at times. You just have to have the discipline to reign in that anxiousness and not go with the lemmings over the cliff."

Yet, members of the Global Manufacturing Vanguard are demonstrating that they have the tenacity, flexibility, leadership, and ability to stay the course. They know there is no finish line to cross, only a pack of challengers of which it must stay ahead. Says Chrysler Executive Vice President Dennis Pawley, "There's no use asking when this will be over, because it's never over. It's a marathon. You can't win it, you can only lose it if you give up."

Notes

Chapter 2

[1] William M. Carley, "Charging Ahead: To Keep GE's Profits Rising, Welch Pushes Quality Control Plan," *Wall Street Journal*, January 13, 1997, 1A.

[2] Gail Schares, "Mr. Barnevik, Aren't You Happy Now?" *Business Week*, September 27, 1993, 128.

[3] Martha T. Moore, "Execs with Global Vision," *USA Today*, February 8, 1996, 1B.

[4] Jay Branegan, *Time*, February 24, 1997, 32, international edition.

[5] Rich Karlgaard, "Percy Barnevik," *Forbes*, December 5, 1994.

Chapter 3

[1] Information on TPS is drawn from the book *The Toyota Pro-*

duction System, second edition (Toyota, 1996), and from conversations with members of the staff of the Supplier Support Center, Georgetown, Kentucky.

[2] Greg Gardner, "The Cloud Over Chrysler's Quality," *Ward's Auto World,* June 1996.

Chapter 4

[1] Since this interview in March, 1996, Manvel has been assigned to Chrysler's plant in Venezuela.

Chapter 5

[1] Stanley Reed, "New Company, Same Ambition: Build a Global Giant," *Business Week,* May 12, 1997, 60.

[2] Justin Martin, "Mercedes: Made in Alabama," *Fortune,* July 7, 1997, 150–58.

[3] David Stamp, "Mercedes-Benz Sows a Learning Field," *Training,* June 1997, 1B.

[4] Ibid.

[5] James R. Healey, "Mercedes Bends Rules," *USA Today,* July 16,1997, 1B.

[6] Ibid.

[7] David Lamb, "American Album," *Los Angeles Times,* December 19, 1996, A5, home edition.

[8] Matt Hamblen, "Mill Disaster Fires Up Planned IS Overhaul," *Computerworld,* January 20, 1997, 1.

Chapter 6

[1] Williams was offered a job by Toyota in September 1997, and is scheduled to begin work at the plant in early 1998.

Chapter 7

[1] Reuters News Service, January 2, 1997.

[2] *Nurturing Global Leadership* (Chicago: A. T. Kearney Executive Search, 1995).

Chapter 8

[1] Milan Brahmbhatt, *Global Economic Prospects and the Developing Countries* (World Bank Press Release 98/1454, 1997).

[2] Jim Rohwer, "Asia's Tigers," *Fortune*, October 17, 1997, 134.

[3] Micheline Maynard and James R. Healey, "BMW's Big Gamble," *USA Today*, September 24, 1997, 1B.

[4] Hamish McRae, *The World in 2020* (Boston: Harvard Business School Press, 1994).

Bibliography

Collins, James C. and Jerry I. Porras. *Built to Last.* New York: HarperBusiness, 1997; HarperCollins, 1994.

Greider, William. *One World, Ready or Not.* New York: Simon & Schuster, 1997.

Hamel, Gary and C. K. Prahalad. *Competing for the Future.* Boston: Harvard Business School Press, 1994.

Ingrassia, Paul and Joseph B. White. *Comeback.* New York: Simon & Schuster, 1995.

Maynard, Micheline. *Collision Course.* New York: Birch Lane Press, 1995.

McRae, Hamish. *The World in 2020,* Boston: Harvard Business School Press, 1994.

Morrison, Terri, Wayne A. Conaway, and Joseph J. Douress. *Dun & Bradstreet's Guide to Doing Business around the World.* New York: Prentice Hall, 1997.

211

Schwartz, Peter. *The Art of the Long View.* New York: Doubleday, 1991.

Wilms, Wellford. *Restoring Prosperity.* New York: Times Business, 1996.

Womack, James and Daniel T. Jones. *Lean Thinking.* New York: Simon & Schuster, 1996.

Womack, James, Daniel T. Jones, and Daniel Roos. *The Machine That Changed the World.* New York: Rawson Associates, 1990.

Index